Structural Interpretation of Seismic Data

Robert E. Sheriff
University of Houston

Originally presented at an AAPG
Continuing Education course for the
Dallas Geological Society, February 1981.

Acknowledgements

This paper was prepared for an
American Association of Petroleum Geologists
Continuing Education course presented for the
Dallas Geological Society February 1981.

Extra copies of this and all other books in the AAPG Education
Course Note Series are available from:

AAPG Bookstore
P.O. Box 979
Tulsa, Oklahoma 74101 – 0979

Published July 1982
Third Printing, January 1986
ISBN: 0 – 89181 – 172 – 9

Structural Interpretation of Seismic Data

I. <u>Relation of structural section to seismic section</u>

The picture in Fig. 1 shows the result of dropping a pebble into the very calm water of a mountain lake in the early morning. The impact of the pebble sent out waves. The nature of the source was a bit complex because when the pebble hit the water it sent up a few water droplets, which subsequently impacted on the surface and generated a complex waveform. Part of the expanding wave train struck the shore, in this case a large rock, and was reflected. There are differences between the reflected waveform and the

Fig. 1.   Waves on the surface of a mountain lake, resulting from dropping a pebble into the water. (From Sheriff, 1980b).

direct waveform. The slope and contrast at the reflecting rock modified the reflecting waveform. The problem analogous to the seismic interpretational problem is to deduce the shape and nature of the rock surface from observations of the reflected waveform. To do that, we deal with the complications of wave theory. Note that the reflected waveform is not exactly the same shape as the reflector. For example, near the center of the reflected wave is an interference pattern where reflections from different parts of the reflecting surface arrive at the same time.

Modern seismic processing makes seismic sections look so much like cross sections through the earth that we are tempted to interpret them as that. In some ways this is a useful way of thinking. However, a seismic section is not a simple slice through the earth. Fig. 2 shows a model of a faulted anticline. Let us determine the seismic section which would represent this earth model. This problem is the opposite of the one we usually face, which is deducing the nature of the earth from a seismic section.

We want to determine the common-depth-point stacked seismic section, which would result from a seismic line shot across Fig. 2. First, consider acquisition techniques. Today, most seismic sections are made by the common-depth-point technique. We observe reflected (and other) waves from a number of sources with a number of detectors, giving a large number of input traces. We arrange the observed input traces so those with a common midpoint are grouped together; this is called a common midpoint gather.

For example (Fig. 3), for a flat reflector without involving velocity complications, the waves from source A recorded by geophone 1 might involve reflecting point A1. Another source B recorded by another geophone 2 might involve the same reflecting point. Many combinations of source and receiver involve the same reflecting point. In processing, we correct arrival times to what would have been observed for the path from a source at the midpoint to the reflector and back to a detector located at the midpoint. Adjust the arrival times to find what would have resulted with a coincident source and receiver located midway between each actual source and detector, and then

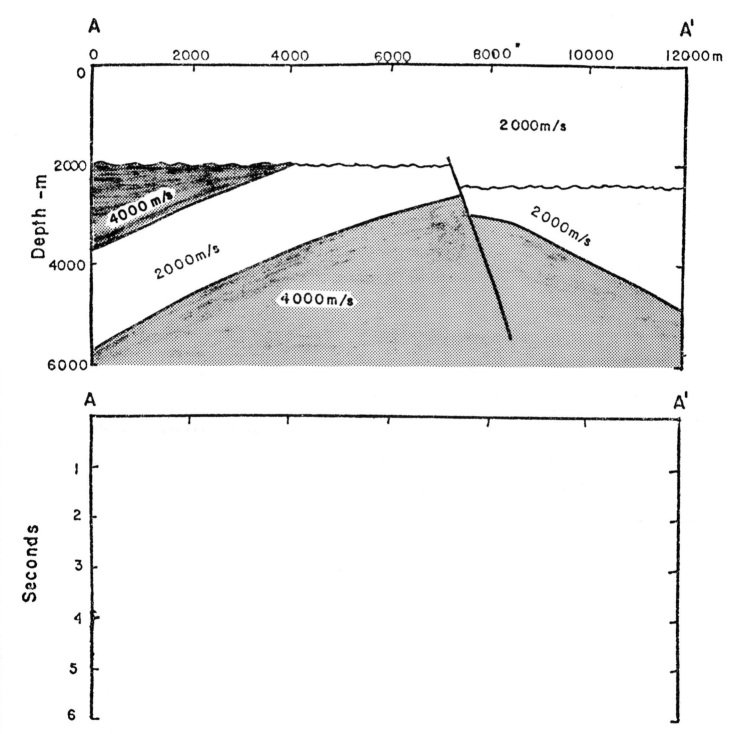

Fig. 2. Model of a faulted anticline. The problem: sketch below it the arrival times of events on a common-depth-point section which might be shot across it. (From Sheriff, 1978.)

combine all traces that involve the same midpoint to make one output trace on the seismic section. Thus a common-depth-point stacked section shows the calculated effect of having a source, and a receiver, coincident with each other for each trace (although that is not the arrangement actually used to record the data). With sources and detectors coincident, travel paths back from a reflector retrace the travel paths down to the reflector and the travel path strikes the final reflector at right angles.

Some of the elements for the traces are missing toward the end of the seismic line. Consequently, there is a taper region at each end of a seismic line that involves the stacking of fewer elements. The noise content of these portions is usually higher and the interpretation more difficult. For typical seismic lines, this region of degraded quality covers the same distance as the spread length. Thus for a 3-km spread, it affects the last 3 km at the end of each line. Short lines are often inferior to long lines because a larger proportion of the line is affected. Sometimes similar effects occur elsewhere because of difficulties in the field, access or permit problems, etc.

The geophysicist measures the arrival time of reflections. For the

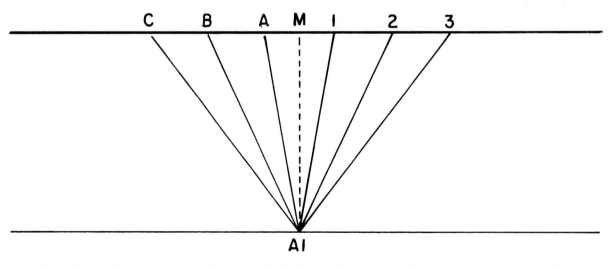

Fig. 3. Arrangement for acquisition of common-depth-point data. Reflections from a source at A received by a geophone at 1, from B to 2, and from C to 3. All involve the same reflecting point A1 and are referenced to the same midpoint M.

first reflector (the top of the 4,000 m/sec (13,200 ft/sec) wedge) shown in Fig. 2, the energy travels 2,000 m (6,600 ft) to the reflector and 2,000 m (6,600 ft) coming back up: a total travel distance of 4,000 m (13,200 ft). The velocity is specified as 2,000 m/sec (6,600 ft/sec), which gives a travel time of 2 seconds, so we plot a reflection at 2 seconds on Fig. 4. Much of the energy reaching a reflector passes right through it. Travel paths which pass through interfaces where the velocity changes are bent according to Snell's law:

$$\frac{\text{sine of angle of incidence}}{\text{sine of angle refraction}} = \frac{\text{velocity in incident medium}}{\text{velocity in refracting medium}}$$

Fig. 5 illustrates this with a reflection from the base of a high-velocity wedge. The angle between the reflections on the seismic time section (Fig. 6) will differ from the angle between the reflectors because of velocity changes, as well as the scale ratio employed in plotting the data and other factors. The farthest point to the right from which a reflection

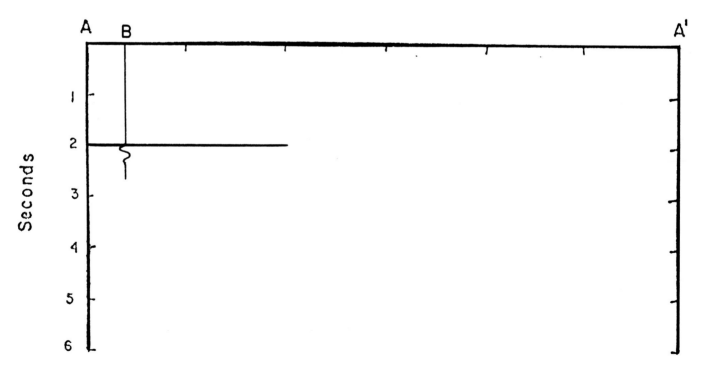

Fig. 4. Reflection from top of high-velocity wedge in Fig. 2, shown as line indicating its arrival time and also on the seismic trace at point B.

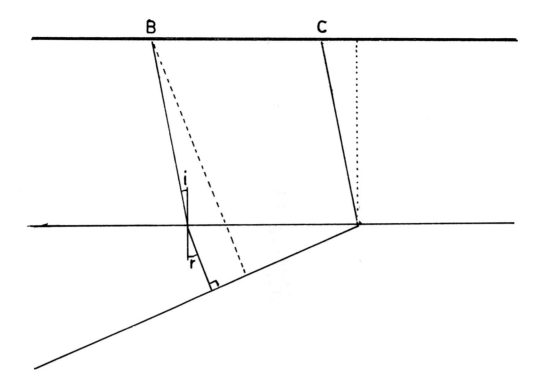

Fig. 5. A raypath from a point on the surface B is bent on passing through an interface where the velocity changes. Travel by the solid line is quicker than by the shorter dashed line. The angle of incidence is i, the angle of refraction is r.

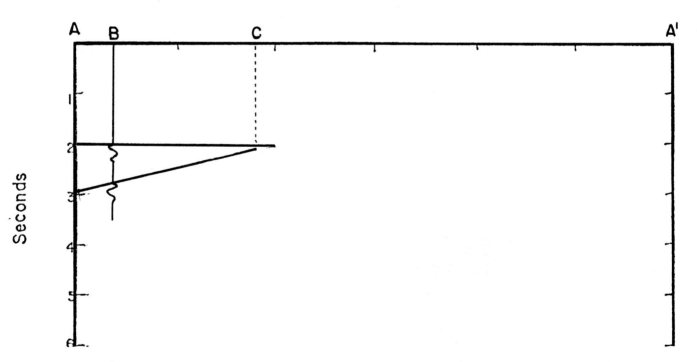

Fig. 6. Reflections from top and base of high-velocity wedge in Fig. 2, shown as lines indicating their arrival time and also on the seismic trace at point B.

(from the bottom of the high-velocity wedge)can be obtained is C (on Figs. 5 and 6). Beyond this the energy is all diffraction energy.

The amplitude of reflections involves the boundary conditions at interfaces. There are several boundary conditions to be satisfied; specifically the continuity of displacement and the continuity of stress. Impossibilities result if displacement and stress are not continuous. Expressing these conditions as equations permits us to determine the amplitude of the reflected wave in terms of the physical properties on opposite sides of the interface. The final equations are complicated in the general case where the interface can be approached from different directions. However, for an approach at right angles to the interface, the expression is fairly simple. The amplitude of the reflected wave compared to the amplitude of the incident wave is given by the change in the product of the density and velocity, as shown:

$$\text{Reflectivity} = \frac{\text{amplitude of reflected wave}}{\text{amplitude of incident wave}}$$

$$= \frac{\text{change in product of velocity and density}}{\text{twice average product of velocity and density.}}$$

Where the change in velocity is from 2,000 to 4,000 m/sec (as at the top of the high-velocity wedge) with no change in density, we have a reflectivity of one-third, meaning that the reflected wave has one-third the amplitude of the incident wave. The fraction of the energy reflected is proportional to the square of the reflectivity, so the energy reflected is one-ninth of the incident energy. This means that eight-ninths of the energy travels right through the interface. The contrasts in this model (from 2,000 to 4,000 m/sec) were chosen to make the calculations easy. They are much larger than most contrasts in the actual earth, where contrasts would more likely involve a

100 m/sec (330 ft/sec) change than a 2,000 m/sec (6,600 ft/sec) change. The actual reflectivity at most interfaces is very small, often of the order of 0.01. Hence the fraction of the energy reflected is usually minute (0.01% in this case), and almost all of the energy (99.99%) is transmitted. This is fortunate because then the transmitted energy is available to be reflected from deeper interfaces.

At the base of the high-velocity wedge in Fig. 2, the terms in the numerator are reversed with respect to what they are at the top of the wedge where the velocity change was +200. At the base of the high-velocity wedge, the change is -200, giving a reflectivity of -1/3. The minus sign in the reflection coefficient inverts the seismic wavelet. The magnitude of the reflectivity is the same. If we also ignore the slight loss of energy in passing through the top of the wedge, and assume that corrections were made for spherical divergence and other types of energy losses (operations normally carried out in data processing), the reflection amplitude is the same. If the incident waveform is a trough followed by a peak, then the waveform from the upper interface is a trough followed by a peak; but that from the lower interface is inverted in polarity, that is, a peak followed by a trough. From the amplitude we learn about the degree of contrast present at the interface, and from the polarity we learn whether the change goes from lower to higher, or higher to lower.

In this model, we imply no changes in density. Density is a factor in reflectivity but often density changes are not known. In the earth, density and velocity often change in the same direction, and normally an increase in velocity implies an increase in density. At the portion of the unconformity where there is no change in the product of velocity and density, the reflectivity is zero and there is no reflection. However, there are usually changes in properties at an unconformity and usually an unconformity gives rise to a strong reflection. In fact, the strongest reflections often arise from unconformities.

The unconformity is shown as a wavy line, by convention. However, we might think of the wavy line as indicating a rough surface and ask what the roughness implies with respect to the reflection. The answer depends upon the wavelengths of the seismic energy, as it does in many different problems; such as whether a thin bed generates a reflection, whether we can resolve the reflections from the top and bottom of a bed, or whether a structure gives an indication of sufficient magnitude to see.

Wavelength is usually expressed as the quotient of the velocity and frequency. This simple equation is also expressed in the nomogram of Fig. 7. When dealing with reflections from the shallow part of the section (depths of 1 to 2 km), the velocity is often low (about 2 km/sec or 6,600 ft/sec), and reflections of moderately high frequency (about a dominant frequency of 50 hertz) giving a wavelength of 40 m (about 135 ft). A rule of thumb (the Rayleigh resolvable limit) is that features need to be larger than about one-quarter wavelength to be seen properly. Such a value is about 10 m (35 ft) in this instance. Features smaller than this are very difficult to see. As we go deeper in the earth the velocity generally increases and the frequency decreases. Assuming at depth a velocity of 5 km/sec (about 16,400 ft/sec), and a frequency of 20 hertz, the wavelength is 250 m (about 820 ft). The one-quarter wavelength rule then means a deep feature 60 m (200 ft) in physical dimension has the same seismic expression as a 10 m (35 ft) feature much shallower. The range of wavelengths on seismic sections is about ten to one. If we assume, for example, that the section was faulted after deposition with a throw of about 30 m (100 ft), at shallow depths the 30 m

(100 ft) throw is much larger than a one-quarter wavelength and the fault

shows clearly. At greater depths the 30 m (100 ft) becomes small compared to

a one-quarter wavelength, and the fault appears to die out with depth.

The terminus of the high velocity wedge sends energy back as a

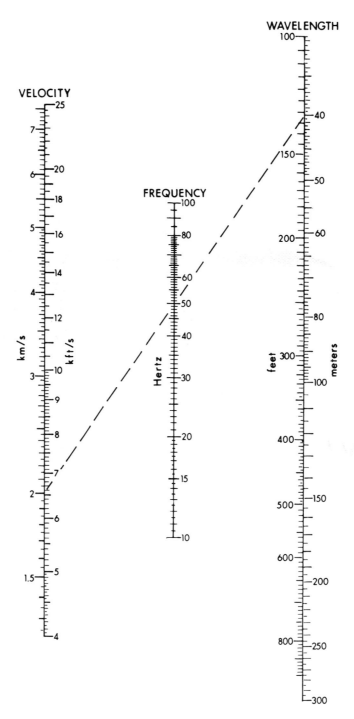

Fig. 7. Nomogram; a straight line relates velocity, frequency, and
wavelength. The two outside scales give metric values, the inner scales
English ones. Example: for velocity = 2km/s and frequency = 50 Hz, the
wavelength = 40 m. (From Sheriff, 1980a.)

diffraction. The diffraction is observed at many points and Fig. 8 shows

raypaths to two points. We can track raypaths for as many points as

necessary to define the shape of the diffraction curve. Diffractions are

very useful in interpretation because the crest of the diffraction curve

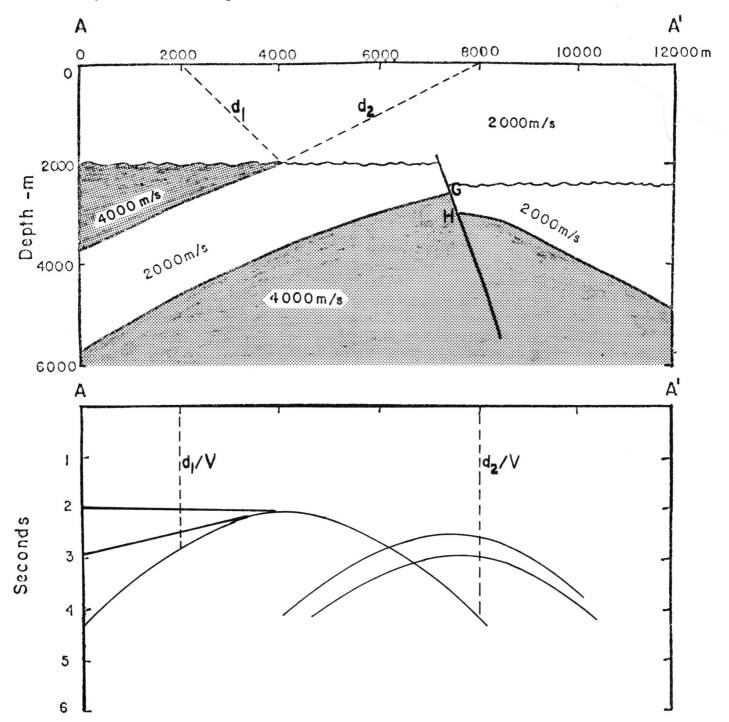

Fig. 8.   Diffraction from the point of the high-velocity wedge. Two
possible raypaths are shown in the upper diagram and the diffraction
arrival time in the lower. Diffractions from points G and H are also
shown.

locates the discontinuity. Diffractions are especially useful in picking

faults. The point where reflections terminate is often not clear because the

reflections blend into diffractions and reflections are seen from the downdip

direction rather than at the reflector location on an unmigrated section. But

the crest of the diffraction locates the fault correctly.

The migration process collapses diffractions back to the point at the crest.

The reflection from the top of the wedge and the reflection from the bottom

of the wedge are tangent to the diffraction curve. In general, reflections

are tangent to the diffraction curve associated with the terminus of the

reflectors.

Diffractions are also generated at the points (G and H on Fig. 8) where

the basement reflectors truncate against the fault. The reflections which

terminate at those points are tangent to the diffractions. The reflections

are continuous with diffractions both in amplitude and in phase, so it is not

clear where the change from a reflection into a diffraction occurs.

While the top of the basement on the model is continuous and smooth, the

reflection from it has a kink (and actually some overlap) because of

distortion by the overlying high-velocity wedge (which acts as a distorting

lens). We can imagine two raypaths involving reflecting points E and F not

very far apart on this reflector, as illustrated in Fig. 9. The raypath from

E back to the surface may not encounter the high-velocity wedge, whereas the

one from F may be sent by the high-velocity wedge so that it crosses the

raypath from E. This type of complication can occur where there is a lateral

variation of velocity, and it involves distortion of events below the lateral

variation. Thus the basement event is distorted because of the shallower

wedge. Over the portion of the surface P the basement reflection is observed

twice, once without going through the wedge and once going through the wedge,

producing a multiple-branch situation.

Such a situation also produces "phantom" diffractions (Fig. 9). They are real diffractions in that we see them on the seismic section and they are phantom only in the sense that there is no discontinuity in the reflecting interface associated with them.

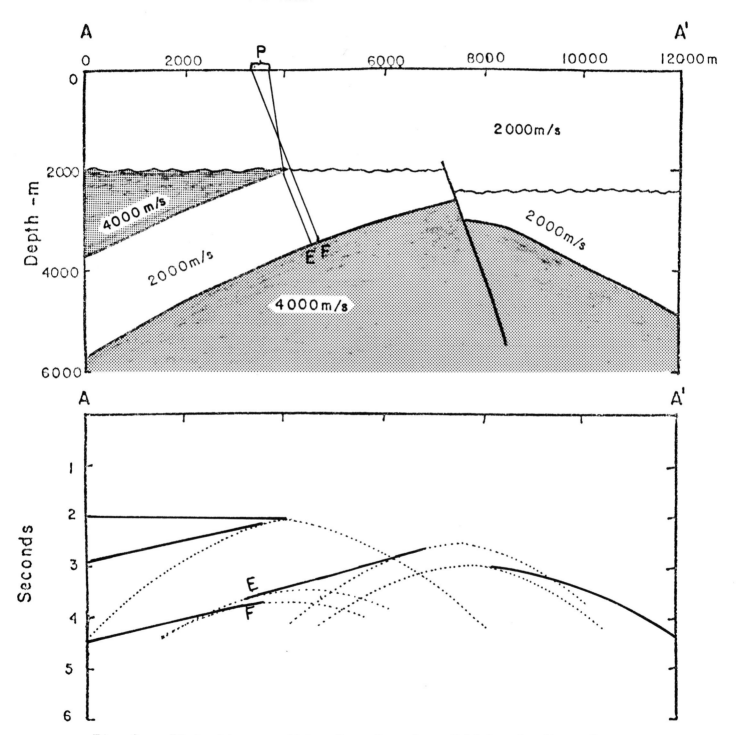

Fig. 9. Distortion resulting from focusing of high-velocity wedge. Raypaths from E and F will cross in the subsurface because of bending of raypath from E by the high-velocity wedge. Over the region P dual reflections will be seen.

This situation of multiple branches results whenever seismic rays pass through a focal point before reaching the recording surface. In physical optics the crossing of light rays is called a focus and the phenomena involved here is called velocity focusing. The high-velocity wedge acts as a lens to bring seismic raypaths to a focus.

The contrast between G and H on Fig. 8, associated with the fault, should produce a fault plane reflection. However, because of the steep dip of the fault plane, the observation points for such a reflection are displaced an appreciable distance to the right and in this instance are beyond the right end of the seismic line. The travel paths for the fault plane reflection are fairly long and the arrival time may be beyond the times at which we look. In this instance, the fault plane reflection occurs after 7 seconds and would probably not be observed (because records are usually cut off at 6 seconds) even if the line was long enough. Often we do not recognize fault plane reflections because we do not look for them in the right place. We also discriminate against them because of the directivity of detector arrays. Usually the best way to locate fault planes is by diffraction curves.

A summary of the primary reflection and diffraction events from our model is shown on Fig. 10. In addition, an actual seismic section would show other types of events, such as multiples and noise. Also shown on Fig. 10 are first-order multiples involving the surface and the multiple that bounces within a high-velocity wedge. The effective reflectivity of multiples is found by taking the products of the reflectivity at each of the reflecting interfaces involved: $(1/3)(-1)(1/3)=-1/9$ for the unconformity-surface-unconformity multiple. Generally, the only important multiples are those involving exceptionally strong reflectors. Additional events such as reflected diffractions, diffracted reflections, multiple diffractions, etc., exist, but are usually so weak that they are not identified and merely add to background noise.

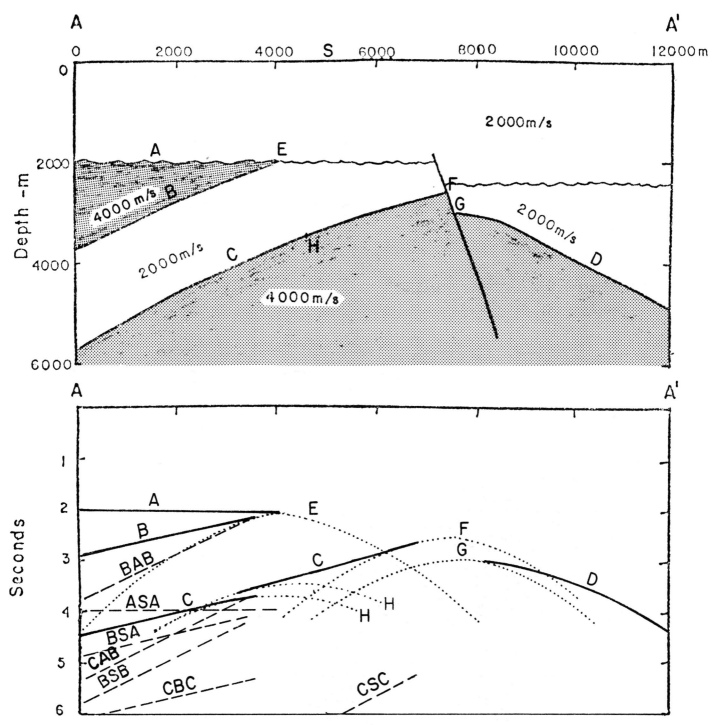

Fig. 10. Arrival time of primary reflections (solid lines) and diffractions (dotted lines). The sources of the reflections and diffractions are indicated by letters keying them to the reflectors and diffracting points above. First-order multiples are also shown (dashed lines) identified by the reflecting interfaces involved.

The portion of the subsurface that we are viewing differs somewhat from the location of the seismic line on the surface, because in this instance it is shorter at both ends. The fact that the portion of the subsurface being mapped differs from that just under the line must be taken into account when planning seismic lines.

The length of a reflection event on a seismic section differs from the length of the reflector when the reflector has a curvature. With anticlinal curvature the reflection is longer than the reflecting interface, so that an anticline looks larger than it really is. However, the reflected energy is spread out over a longer portion of the seismic section, so the reflection from anticlinal curvature is weakened. Correction for curvature effects is automatically made in migration to give the amplitude associated with reflectivity.

The opposite effect results from moderate synclinal curvature: the reflection is spread over a smaller distance and the amplitude is built up. The situation for sharp synclinal curvature is different, as is seen in the next model.

Fig. 11 shows a variation of the model of Fig. 2; it includes an adjacent syncline. Different portions of the syncline are seen from the same surface locations so that multiple branches will appear. Thus from point A on Fig. 12 both right (R) and left (L) flanks are seen as well as a reflection from the curved bottom (B) of the syncline. Where the curvature is more complicated, or if there is also curvature perpendicular to the seismic line, more than three branches are seen. In this instance, the right flank reflection comes from beyond the end of the seismic line, and part of the diffraction from the point P where the right flank is truncated by the unconformity also shows.

The reflection from the curved bottom of the syncline (Fig. 13) is called a "reverse" branch. Its location is found by tracing as many raypaths as necessary to define the shape adequately. These raypaths cross, passing through a buried focus. The reflection has convex-upward curvature; the

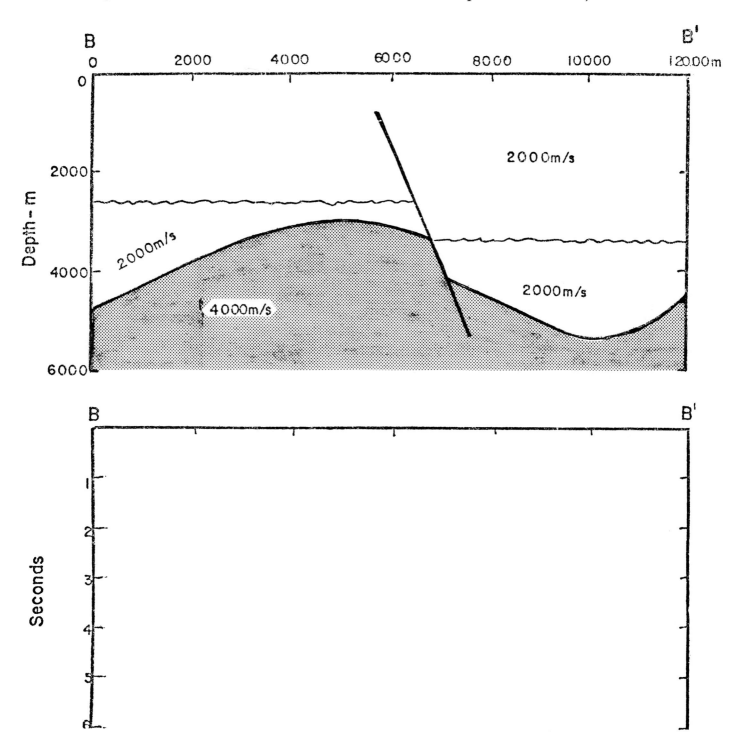

Fig. 11. Model of faulted anticline and syncline. The problem is to sketch the arrival times of events on a common-depth-point section which might be shot across it. (From Sheriff, 1978.)

curvature is reversed. The right side of the reverse branch comes from the left side of the syncline (L), so the sense of direction is also reversed along the reverse branch. A reverse branch occurs when the energy passes through a focal point. This is a case of geometrical focusing; a

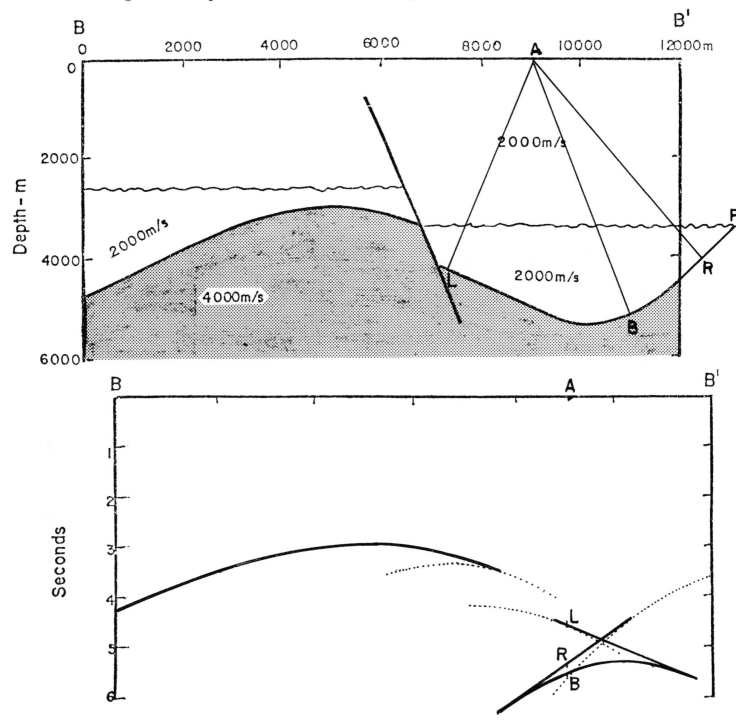

Fig. 12. Primary reflection and diffraction events from the anticline-syncline model. Multiple branches exist to the right, and the same reflector gives rise to more than one reflection at the same observing point. Thus at A one can get reflections from L, R, and B.

curved-mirror effect of the bottom of the syncline produces the focus and inverts the shape of the event.

The result is similar to the phantom diffraction effect which was produced by a velocity "lens". The likelihood of buried-focus phenomena increases with

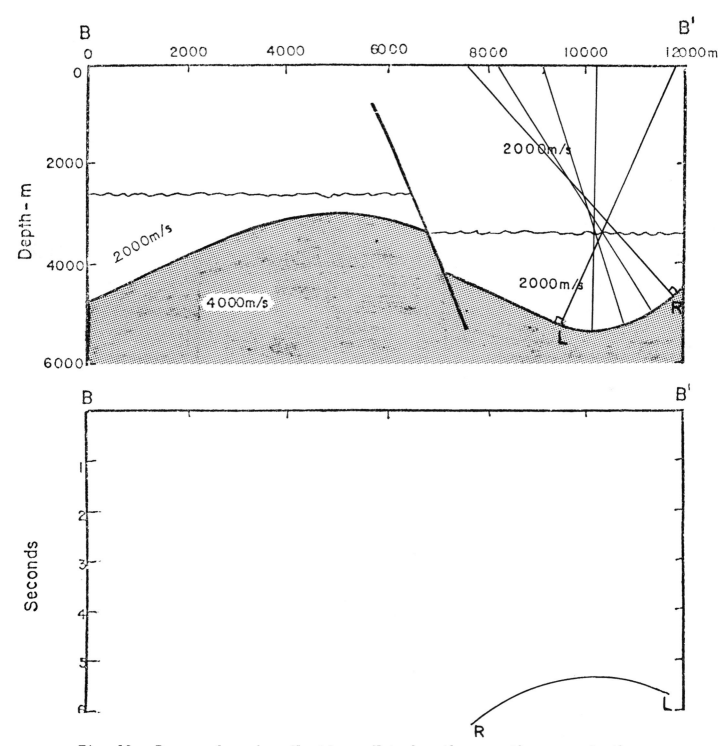

Fig. 13. Reverse-branch reflection. Note how the raypaths cross in the subsurface.

depth, which tends to make the deeper parts of seismic sections more complicated.

In these two models we assumed cylindrical structure (parallel lines involving exactly the same features) so we would not have to be concerned with data coming from outside the vertical cross section containing the seismic line. In the actual earth we also have events coming from the sides, and such out-of-plane events introduce further complications.

II. Migration To Remedy Geometric Distortions

Tucker and Yorsten used Fig. 14 as a cover picture for their book, Pitfalls of Seismic Interpretation; a syncline was interpreted as an anticline, a fairly obvious buried-focus effect. The legend, "low, not again," indicates that past failures were due to a lack of understanding of seismic principles and geometric effects. I imagine most geophysicists and geologists recall instances of very costly errors because of naive interpretations.

In this section, I examine techniques for correcting the geometrical distortions showed in the previous section. "Migration" is the name given to such techniques, which involves repositioning data elements and changing from a system referenced to the observing points to a system referenced to the reflector locations. The input to the migration process is a seismic section oriented to the midpoints between shot and geophone locations, and the output is a seismic section oriented to where discontinuities and various features are located in the earth.

The first seismic section plotted by Karcher on August 9, 1921, involved migration (Fig. 15). This seismic line was shot in Oklahoma and reflections were recorded at different locations from the contact between the Sylvan shale and the Viola limestone, where there is a large contrast, which resulted in a large distinctive reflection. Karcher realized that the reflections were not coming from vertically underneath his observing points. He struck arcs appropriate to the travel times of the reflections at the different locations and regarded the common tangent to those arcs as the reflecting interface. The idea of striking wavefronts, which is in effect what he was doing, came to be called the "common-tangent" method of migration. It was rediscovered a number of years after Karcher used it in 1921. The method is still appropriate if we allow for velocity variations in plotting the wave fronts, rather than simply striking arcs as Karcher did (in

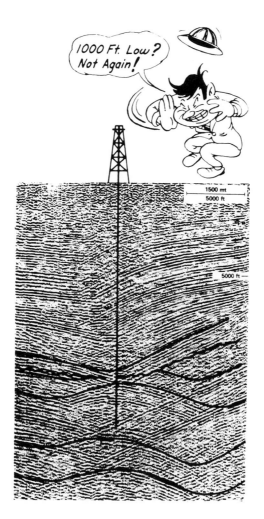

Fig. 14. Cover picture from Tucker and Yorsten, 1973. The misinterpretation is of reverse branches on an unmigrated section.

effect assuming constant velocity, which in his case was not a bad assumption).

Some migration methods are:

swinging wave fronts (common-tangent method)

use of wave fronts and raypaths (including use of various

plotting arm devices, and timing along raypaths)

conjunctive use of wave fronts with diffraction curves

(after Hagedoorn, 1954)

migrating diffraction curves to their crests, including

diffraction stack and Kirchhoff migration

wave-equation migration (finite-difference migration and

frequency-domain migration of several kinds).

This list is rather arbitrary and methods could be grouped differently. For example, all the methods could be considered "wave-equation" methods.

The wave-front raypath methods involve using combinations of arrival time (which gives the wave front) and differences in arrival time at nearly

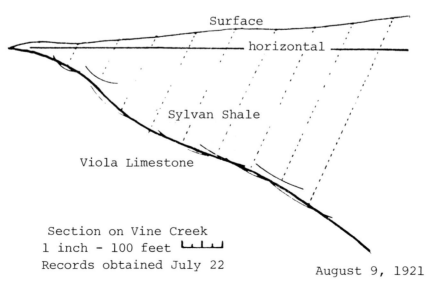

Fig. 15. First seismic line plotted by Karcher in 1921, involving migration. (From Schreiver, 1952.)

detectors (which gives the direction of arrival of the reflected energy and hence the raypath) to locate the reflector. Before computer processing, this operation was carried out long hand by a computer (a person who computes) on the field crew. He often had plotting arms or templates to aid in carrying out this process. A common method was to mount a transparent wave-front chart on a light table (Fig. 16) and overlay translucent graph paper on which the migrated section was plotted. The raypath gave the direction, we counted down along the raypath until we reached the wave front for the reflection arrival time, and we drew a line there to indicate the reflector.

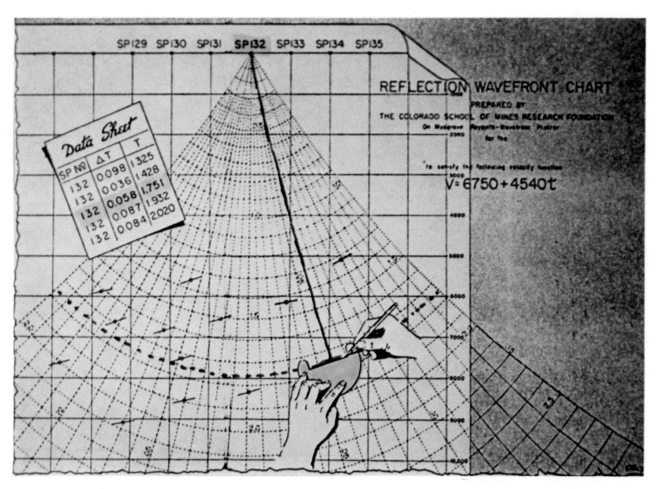

Fig. 16. Migration using a wave-front chart on a light table. The section to be plotted was laid over the wave-front chart with the shotpoint at the chart's apex. The reflector was plotted at the intersection of the raypath, showing the proper difference in arrival time between nearby geophones and the wave front showing the arrival time. (From Musgrave, 1952.)

24

About 1954, Hagedoorn published a paper on the properties of diffraction curves, which gave considerable insight into migration. Hagedoorn showed the relationship between wave-front and diffraction curves. When superimposed properly (Fig. 17), a wave-front and a diffraction curve intersect at two locations; the reflection, which is tangent to the diffraction curve, and the reflector, which is tangent to the wave-front curve. The application of Hagedoorn's concepts to migration were not appreciated at first. It took about 15 years before automatic migration became available (1969) but the technique was based on Hagedorn's ideas. Today, we generally call this

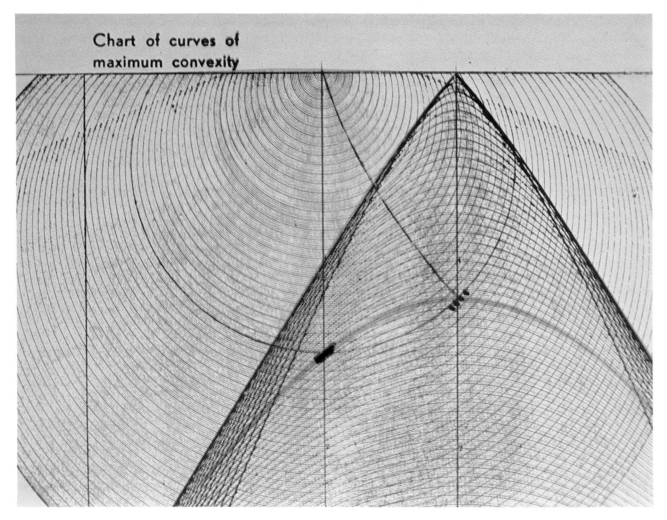

Fig. 17. Superposition of charts showing wave fronts and diffraction curves. When properly aligned, a diffraction curve is tangent to the reflection in its unmigrated position and the reflector is tangent to the wave front chart, each location being at the intersection of the same diffraction and wave-front curves. (After Hagedoorn, 1954.)

method Kirchhoff migration because we use the Kirchhoff diffraction equation. It involved the search for diffractions and moving all the energy along the diffraction curve to the crest of the curve. The technique involves searching along all possible diffraction curves and it was a fairly expensive way to automatically migrate data, but it migrated full waveforms whereas prior methods involved picking reflections and then migrating the picks.

Another full waveform method developed from the idea of swinging wave fronts; each data element was simply "smeared-out" along the wave front for its arrival time. The energy interferes constructively where there is a reflector, but otherwise interferes destructively at random. The operations of summing along diffraction curves and smearing along wave fronts are actually equivalent operations. They involve summing identical data elements, but this was not realized until later.

About 1975 the technique of "wave-equation" migration using the scalar wave equation was developed. By applying the adjective "scalar" we ignore shear waves, but, with the recording geometry most commonly used, shear waves are not abundant so this is not particularly limiting. The wave-equation techniques used a finite-difference method in order to downward continue the seismic wave field. The operation was carried out in the time-space domain and is often called "time-domain" migration. Today, we look back at the early techniques, such as the swinging of wave fronts, and recognize that they were also solutions of the wave equation, except solving the problem in a different form.

We also solve the wave equation in other ways, such as transforming into the frequency versus wave-number domain, carrying out equivalent operations in that domain, and then transforming back. There are several variations of "frequency-domain" solutions. A seismic section has two dimensions: a horizontal dimension measured in distance, and a vertical dimension measured in travel time. We can transform one or the other, or both, of these dimensions to give different types of frequency/wave-number domain solutions.

The various methods of migration are equivalent, or would be equivalent if carried out without making approximations in the solutions. In practical implementations, different approximations are made (and by different processing houses) so there are minor (and sometimes major) differences in the migrated products.

The idea with wave-equation migration is downward continuation. Downward continuation was familiar in potential-methods analysis. We continued gravity and magnetic fields (and sometimes electrical or other types of fields) downward to sharpen anomalies, so it seemed reasonable to continue the seismic wave field downward. Fig. 18 shows geophone depth vertically, and a seismic trace that might be observed by a geophone at the surface of the earth is plotted across the top. This model has three reflecting layers, one at about 303 m (1,000 ft), one at about 757 m (2,500 ft), and one at 1,060 m (3,500 ft), and we assumed a constant velocity of 1,515 m/sec (5,000 ft/sec). The reflector at 303 m (1,000 ft) produces a reflection after a travel path of 606 m (2,000 ft) and so is observed at 0.4 seconds. Likewise, the reflector at 757 m (2,500 ft) gives a reflection at 1.0 second and the one at 1,060 m (3,500 ft), at 1.4 seconds. If we could bury geophones in the earth at various depths, we would see events sharper and less diffuse as the geophones get closer to reflecting interfaces. There would then be less opportunity for reflection and diffraction energy to spread out, so the energy would be concentrated at the location of the reflectors or diffracting points. To use an optical analogy, if we make a contact print without being in contact with the negative, we get a blurred picture. This is somewhat like what we see on a seismic section where we recorded a long distance from the features we are trying to image. As the recording plane approaches the object, the image sharpens, and when the recording plane is in coincidence with the object the picture is in sharp focus. We cannot physically bury the geophones at various depths, but we can use the wave field that we observe at the earth's surface to calculate the seismic wave field at various levels, utilizing the properties of the continuity of wave fields.

In our model, a geophone at 152 m (500 ft) will see the first reflection 0.1 second earlier than at the surface, or at 0.3 second rather than at 0.4 second; and the down-going wave is seen at 0.1 second rather than at zero

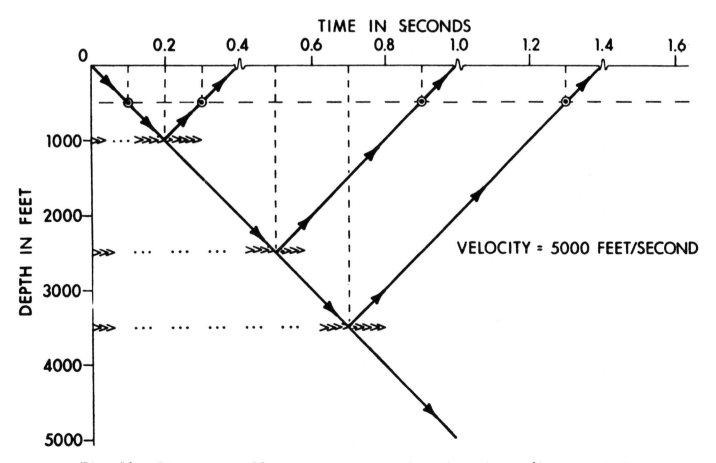

Fig. 18. Diagram to illustrate wave-equation migration. (Courtesy M.T. Taner.)

time when the source is activated. Similarly the other two reflections will be seen at 0.9 second and at 1.3 seconds if the geophone is buried at 303 m (1,000 ft) which is the depth of the first reflector; the down-going wave will be seen at 0.2 second and the reflection, simultaneously, at 0.2 second. The coincidence of down-going and up-going waves tells that a reflector is present at that point. If we dealt with a diffracting point (such as the termination of a reflector), the diffraction would collapse onto the diffracting point, making the termination sharp and locating correctly where the reflector terminates.

Fig. 19 shows a model that includes a gentle syncline, a sharp syncline, a gentle anticline, a sharp anticline, beds which pinchout, beds which infill a basin, isolated diffracting points, and a fault. The model shows the various types of geological features we hope to see on seismic sections. We calculated the seismic section which would have been obtained on a line over

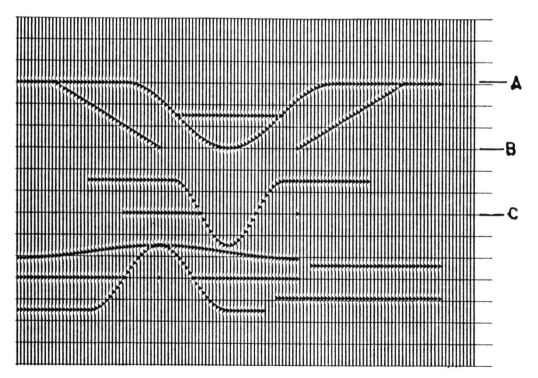

Fig. 19. Model depth section to illustrate wave-equation migration. The velocity is constant in this model. (Courtesy Seiscom-Delta.)

this model (Fig. 20). The model is fairly simple so the section is
sufficiently straightforward and many of the features are clear, although not
necessarily sharp. The nature of the synclines might not be clear,
especially the sharp syncline which involves reverse branches. The
reflections terminate in diffractions which tend to confuse the structural
picture. The location of features like the pinchouts is wrong, because
dipping events are plotted where they are observed on the surface rather than
where the dipping reflectors are actually located. We continue down this
seismic section in steps.

Fig. 21 shows the section continued down to the top of the upper
reflector. We effectively lowered the geophones from the earth's surface
down to a plane which is approximately coincident with the top of the
shallowest feature in the model. By doing so, we sharpened the portions of
the events that are proximate to the observing plane. We also changed the
entire section; note how the bottom of the gentle syncline was rounded and
how the intersection point of the reflections from the flanks of the sharp
syncline moved downward. We continue down to a lower level (Fig. 22) and
then to a still lower level (Fig. 23). Thus we develop a set of sections,
one for each stage of downward continuation. We make a new section of the
portions of these sections that do not overlap (Fig. 24). This gives almost
the original model, differing mainly in disruptions where we go from one
section to another because the steps we took were too coarse. Fig. 25 shows
the same section with steps that are half as big and the continuity is
improved. Fig. 26 is the result of very fine steps, actually used in
processing, and achieves a completely migrated section where events are
plotted in correct locations. We now have a correct structural picture,
subject to several conditions.

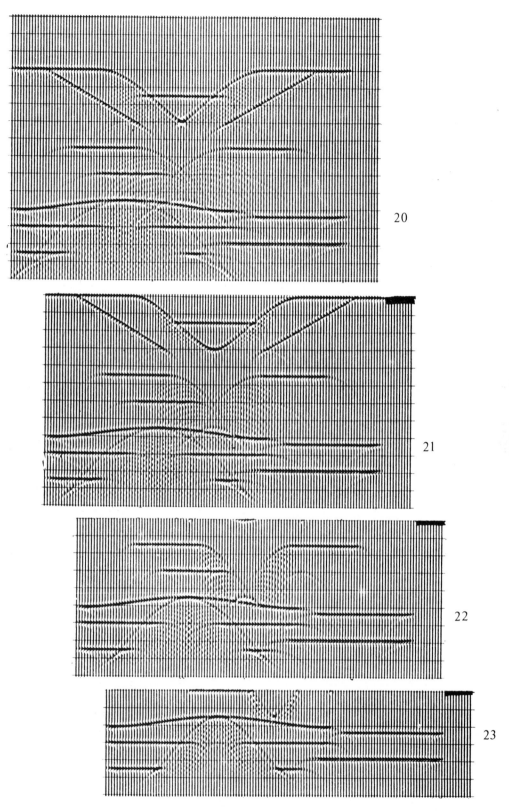

Figs. 20 to 23. Sections to illustrate downward continuation.
Fig. 20 (top) shows the seismic section which would be recorded
across the model shown in Fig. 19. Fig. 21 (next to top) shows
the section which would be recorded with geophones buried at the
depth A in Fig. 19. Fig. 22 (next to bottom) shows the section
which would be recorded at depth B. Fig. 23 (bottom) shows the
section which would be recorded at depth C. (Courtesy Seiscom-Delta.)

Examples of the application of this procedure to real seismic data are shown in the following figures. Fig. 27 shows a seismic section across a syncline. The shallow part is clearly a syncline, but the deeper part shows buried-focus effects. When migrated (Fig. 28), we get a sense of the continuity of the actual synclinal geologic structure. We also achieve more uniformity of amplitude; note the amplitude variation in Fig. 27, particularly that the reverse branches are too strong. Migration corrects the amplitude distortions produced by geometric effects. It also relocates

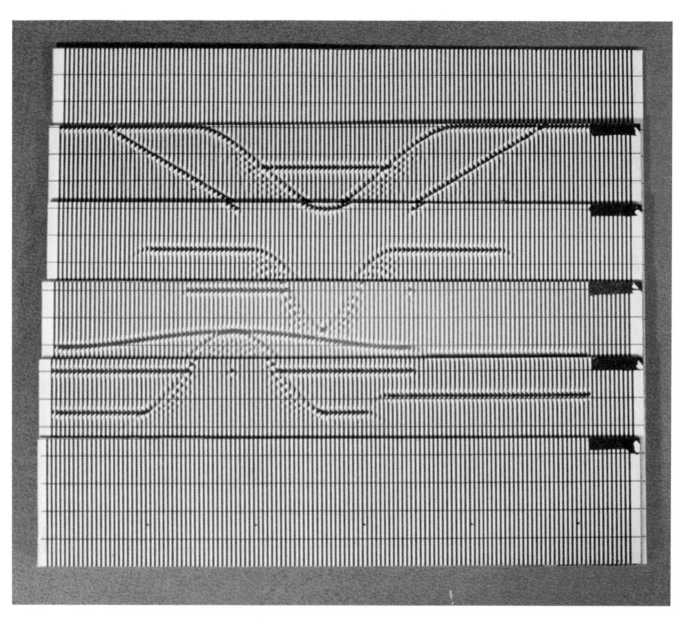

Fig. 24. The sections shown in Figs. 20 to 23 put over each other to yield a migrated section.

32

events. For example, the location of the pinchout P on the migrated section
(Fig. 28) is different from the location on the unmigrated section (Fig. 27).

Fig. 29 shows a seismic section from the Adriatic Sea; we observe
multiple branches that look like synclines, which is what they are. Fig. 30
shows the migrated section. We also see events at the bottom of the seismic
time section (Fig. 29) which were smeared out by the migration (Fig. 30)
so that they look somewhat like wave fronts. Those events were not primary
reflections, as we implicitly assumed when we carried out the migration

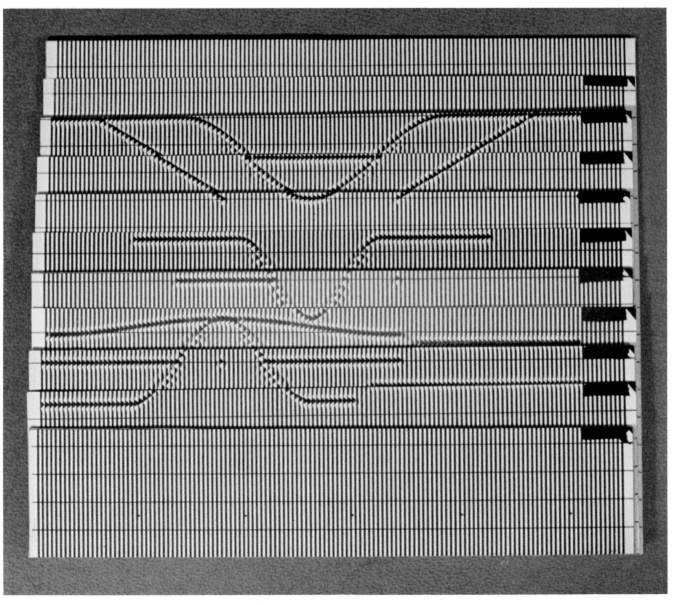

Fig. 25. Same as Fig. 24, except with smaller continuation steps.

process. Migration assumes that all of the data are primary reflections or primary diffractions. In this instance we have taken noise (multiples) and distorted it into a different form. People sometimes call these "smiles." The presence of smiles does not indicate a failure of the migration process, but rather that data were not primary reflection or diffraction data.

Fig. 31 shows a section across an anticline in the Wind River basin. Some faults, probably high-angle reverse faults, are visible but they are not as sharp as we hope for. When we migrate that section (Fig. 32), the anticline becomes smaller in horizontal extent than the unmigrated anticline and reflections terminate more sharply at the faults. Jump correlating across the faults suggests reverse faulting. The void region on our migrated section merely shows that we did not have any information on the unmigrated section for this region. Migration rearranges data, it does not create data. To see what happens in this region we return and get better seismic data,

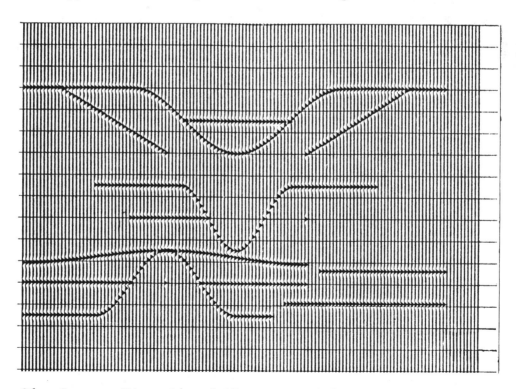

Fig. 26. Same as Figs. 24 and 25, except with very small continuation steps. The result is a migrated section, the image of the model of Fig. 19.

rather than reprocess to improve the migration.

Fig. 33 shows an unmigrated section on the left and a migrated section on the right.   Migration sharpened the fault and it probably can now be

P

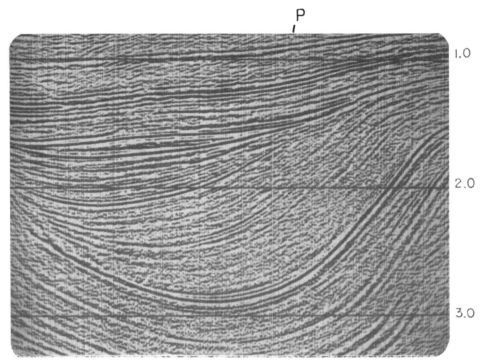

Fig. 27.   Seismic section across a syncline.   (Courtesy Seiscom-Delta.)

P

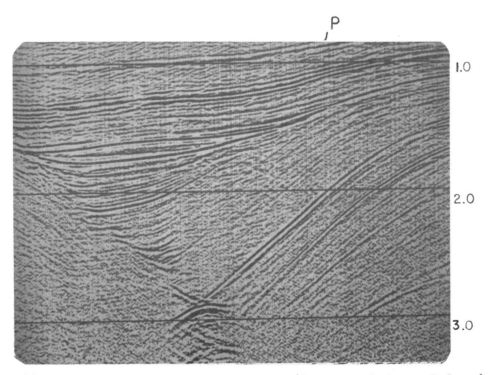

Fig. 28.   Migrated section of Fig. 27.   (Courtesy Seiscom-Delta.)

located within a trace spacing, about 45 m (150 ft) in this instance. Fig.
34 shows another section that involves faulting. We have enough distinction
in the character of events that we could probably jump correlate, indicating
three or so faults of a series of normal faults with fault planes dipping

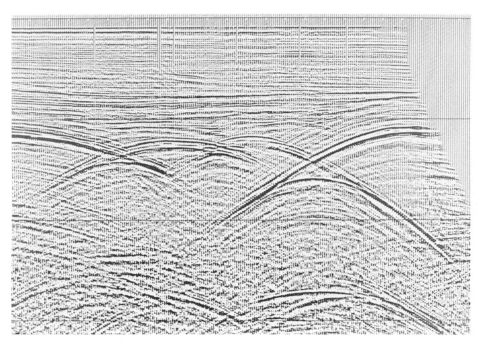

Fig. 29.   Seismic section in the Adriatic Sea.   (Courtesy Seiscom-
Delta.)

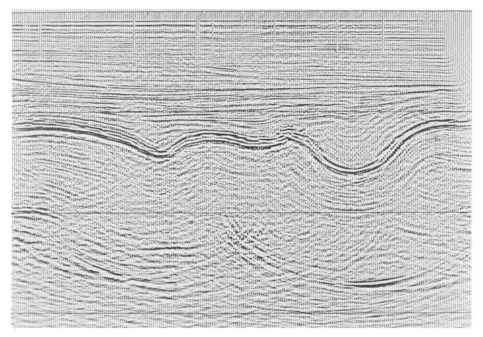

Fig. 30.   Migrated section of Fig. 29.   (Courtesy Seiscom-Delta.)

from left to right. We see many diffractions which we could use to locate the faults, but it is better to migrate (Fig. 35). The faults visible on the unmigrated section now show more clearly and at their correct locations, and we also see a number of other faults which were less evident on the unmigrated section. Migration simplifies the geometric distortions to make interpretation easier.

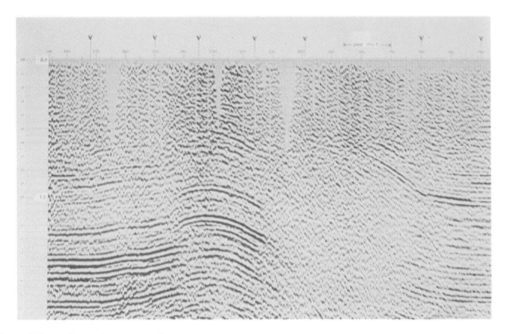

Fig. 31. Section in the Wind River basin. (Courtesy Seiscom-Delta.)

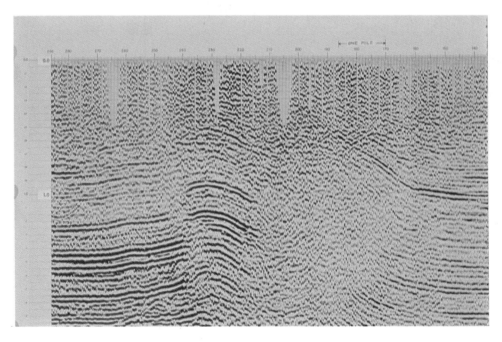

Fig. 32. Migrated section of Fig. 31. (Courtesy Seiscom-Delta.)

Fig. 36 shows a section of almost flat lying data. A few years ago we thought that such flat data did not require migration. However, the data are not all flat, especially the events associated with reflection S. The event S marks the top of a layer of salt and we are dealing with a salt solution edge. Presumably salt was laid over the entire region but subsequently dissolved from part of the region. The salt solution edge sharpens when we see it on the migrated section (Fig. 37). We also see a fairly well-defined fault offsetting the base of the salt; water moving along the fault plane was probably involved with the salt solution. We notice another feature sitting in front of the salt-solution edge; this is a pod of residual salt and it appears to be associated with another fault breaking the base-of-salt

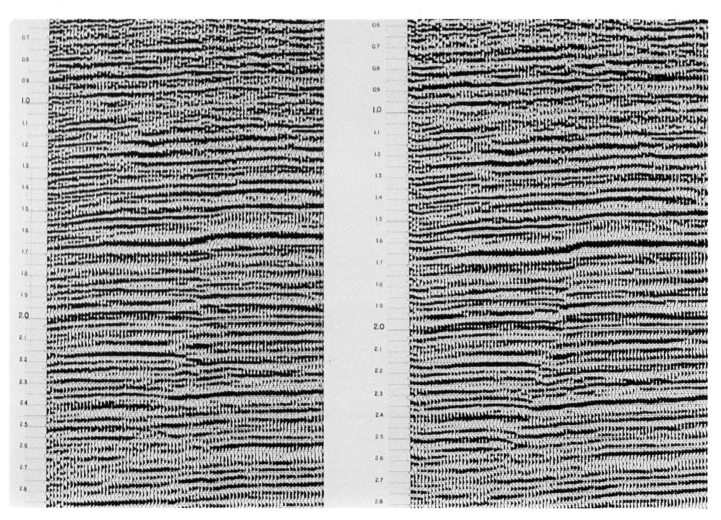

Fig. 33. Unmigrated (left) and migrated (right) sections across a fault. (Courtesy Seiscom-Delta.)

reflector. Since migration does not invent data, these events must be on the

unmigrated section (events A, B on Fig. 36).

This illustrates the importance of migration in sharpening features,

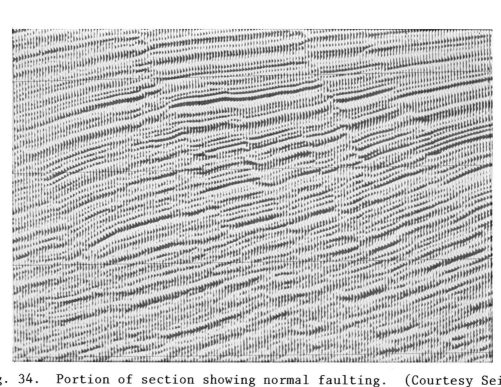

Fig. 34. Portion of section showing normal faulting. (Courtesy Seiscom-Delta.)

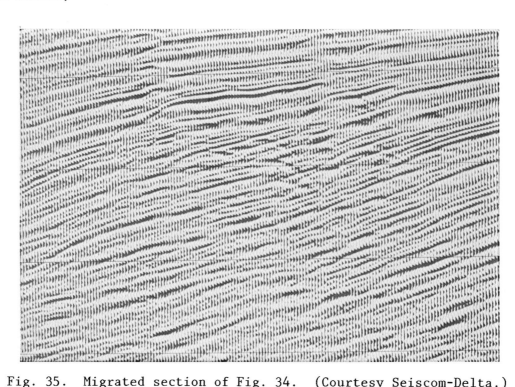

Fig. 35. Migrated section of Fig. 34. (Courtesy Seiscom-Delta.)

especially stratigraphic features, most of which involve angularities in
the seismic data. Since the evidences for stratigraphic features are
displaced from each other, their relationship may not be evident and
relocating the data elements may help clarify features that otherwise might
be missed.

Fig. 38 shows (left) a schematic geologic section, (middle) where events
are seen on a seismic section, and (right) the results of migrating the
seismic section. The migration has recovered structural features, but
geologic sections are usually plotted in depth whereas seismic sections are

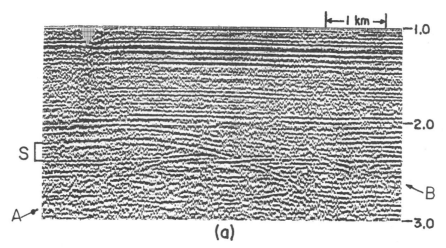

(a)

Fig. 36. Portion of unmigrated section across a salt-solution edge.
(Courtesy Seiscom-Delta.)

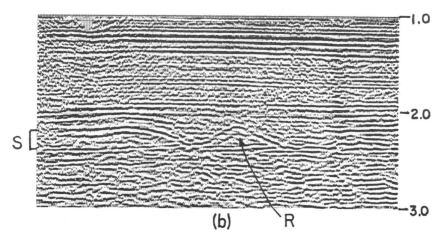

(b)

Fig. 37. Migrated section of Fig. 36. (Courtesy Seiscom-Delta.)

normally plotted in arrival time. Thus, distortions because of the variation

of velocity with depth still remain. I believe we should plot migrated

sections in depth in addition to plotting in time. Geophysicists usually

oppose plotting sections in depth because they realize the uncertainty in our

knowledge of the velocity and its distribution, but we need depth sections

even though they have appreciable uncertainty. A depth section plotted

without vertical exaggeration is a tremendous boon in structural interpretation.

It is important to understand the assumptions made in migrating, because

not all seismic data satisfy them and migration can be misleading (to the

extent that assumptions are not satisfied). Basically, there are three

assumptions:

(1)   that all events are either primary reflections of dif-

fractions; Fig. 30 showed the smiles and other effects

when multiples (or any other type of event that is not

a primary reflection or diffraction) are migrated.

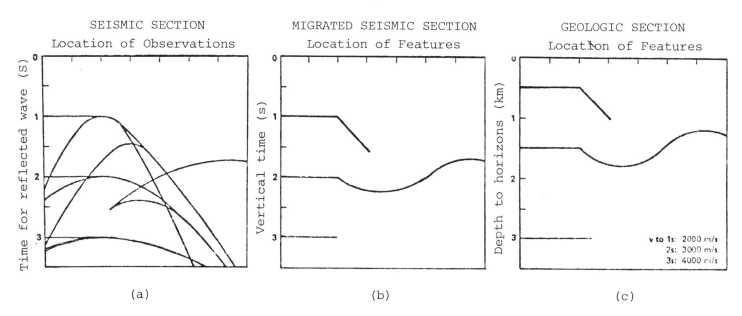

Fig. 38. Comparison of unmigrated and migrated seismic sections with a
geologic section. (a) Arrival times on unmigrated common-depth-point
section; (b) results of migrating (a); (c) geologic section plotted in
depth whereas the seismic sections are plotted in time. (From Sheriff,
1978.)

(2) that no energy comes from the side of the line; we
express this by saying that the data must be "two-dimen-
sional." A parallel seismic line sees exactly the
same picture. This assumption in effect requires that
every seismic line is in the dip direction at every
horizon. Try to imagine a grid of seismic lines, each

(a)

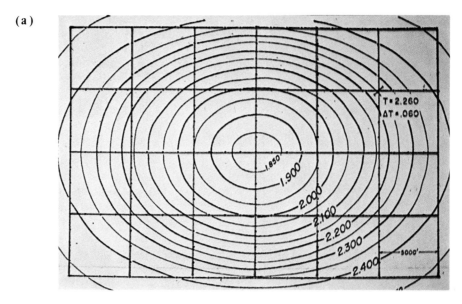

(b)

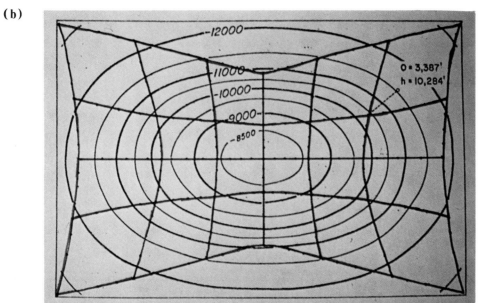

Fig. 39. Diagram illustrating map migration. (a) Map of unmigrated
arrival time over an anticline; (b) result of migrating the map shown in
(a); the anticline has shrunk in area and the rectangular grid of
seismic lines produce a distorted grid tracing the reflection points on
the reflector. (From Musgrave, 1952.)

of which is perpendicular to the strike, and you see the problem. Migration processes the component of dip in the direction of the line, but not the component perpendicular to the line. Usually, the data indicating dip component, perpendicular to the seismic line, are not available. Where we do know the cross dip (which is usually only at line intersections unless we did three-dimensional recording in the field), we can properly allow for this in the migration processes. Ordinarily, this is not done.

(3)   that we know the distribution of velocities. Ordinarily, we allow the velocity to vary only in the vertical direction, according to some velocity function. If the velocity function does not represent the actual velocity distribution correctly, or if the velocity varies horizontally, then a distortion is introduced. We can migrate data properly, including allowing for horizontal changes in velocity, but often we do not know velocity variations to the precision necessary.

One way to solve the third-dimension problem is to first map unmigrated data and then migrate the map. A simple unmigrated anticline is shown in Fig. 39a, and the result of migrating this map is shown in Fig. 39b. The technique for migrating a map is straightforward. Usually, the unmigrated surface is segmented into many small planar pieces which are each migrated according to their respective dips and strikes (to each give a point for the migrated center of the segment) and then the migrated points are recontoured. Note that the projections of the seismic lines onto the mapped horizon (called "sub-surface traces") no longer form a regular grid after migrating.

This is a good migrating technique, except that often we have difficulty following the same seismic event over the entire surface because of interference with different events, and we must make multiple maps where multiple branches occur to apply this technique.

Fig. 40 shows a model with four sharp synclines oriented at different

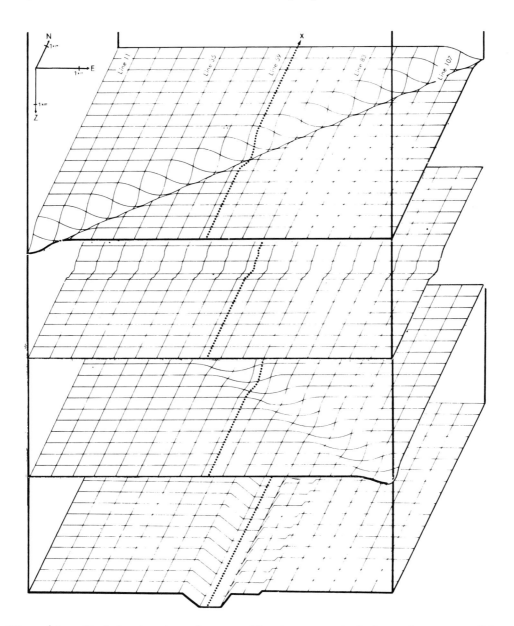

Fig. 40. Model showing four reflectors containing sharp synclines.
(Courtesy Prakla-Seismos.)

angles to the seismic line: 45 degrees for the upper reflector, perpendicular to the seismic line for the second, 45 degrees for the third, and parallel to the seismic line for the lower reflector. Migration is correct for features perpendicular to the line, so the second syncline is migrated correctly, whereas the others are not. Fig. 41 shows the seismic section and Fig. 42 the migrated section. The two synclines at 45 degree angles continue to look like buried-focus events. The syncline that is perpendicular to the seismic line is migrated correctly. The appearance of the syncline parallel with the seismic line is not changed. Where we have violated the assumption that features must be perpendicular to the line, the features have their effects distributed over a smaller region on the migrated section than on the unmigrated. This is one of the big virtues of migration: it usually gives a picture which is more nearly geological than the picture

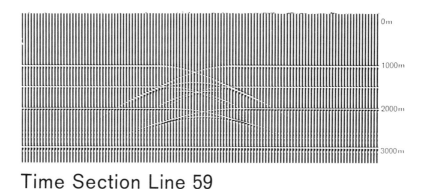

Time Section Line 59

Fig. 41. Unmigrated section across model of Fig. 40. (Courtesy Prakla-Seismos.)

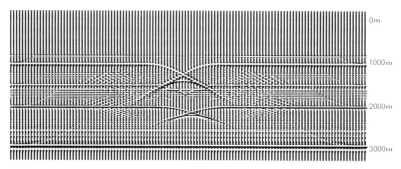

2-D Migrated Depth Section Line 59

Fig. 42. Migrated section of Fig. 41. (Courtesy Prakla-Seismos.)

before, even where the migration assumptions are violated. Migration almost always makes geologic interpretation easier even though the correct solution is not reached.

The uncollapsed buried-focus events on the migrated data on Fig. 42 look 'under-migrated'; the data have not been moved far enough. Under-migration also results from using velocity and velocity gradient values that are too small. Over-migration also results from using velocity values which are too large, although it is less common than under-migration. Instead of bringing the data at A in Fig. 43 to a sharp crest, the data were moved too far.

Now consider the problems in tying seismic data to well data. Fig. 44 shows one small piece of seismic data snipped out of a seismic line and dips from corresponding interfaces observed in a well. Our problem is relating the well data to corresponding events on the seismic section. For this illustration, we ignore possible problems with different datums and the fact

Fig. 43. Example of over-migration. (Courtesy Seiscom-Delta.)

that a seismic event does not even begin until after the two-way travel time
to the reflector, so that "picks" of seismic events are always late with
respect to the travel time to the reflecting interfaces. If the seismic line
is perpendicular to the strike, the obvious way to solve the problem is to
migrate the data as shown in Fig. 45. The solid segments are the seismic

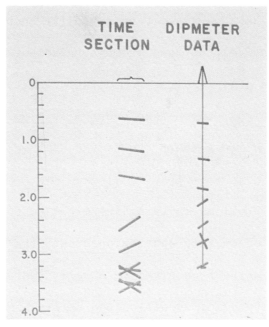

Fig. 44. Diagram showing small vertical slice from a seismic section
and dips determined in a well plotted to the same time scale as the
seismic section. (From Sheriff, 1978.)

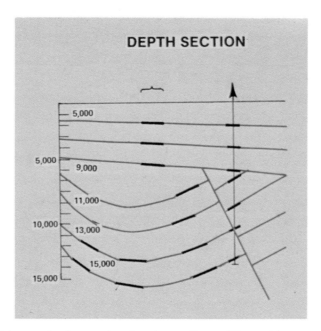

Fig. 45. Migration of the seismic data from Fig. 44 with interpretation
also shown. (From Sheriff, 1978.)

events from Fig. 44 and the intervening structure is filled in with dotted lines. Normally, the whole seismic line will be available so the migrated seismic line will be complete. On the other hand, seismic lines often cannot reach all the way to a well because of fear of damaging the well with explosives, and near the end of a seismic line (for a distance approximately equal to the spread length) quality often deteriorates because the multiplicity decreases.

Occasionally, we are faced with the opposite situation, where our objective is to plan the seismic line such that it ties the well. Often the seismic line is run to the wellhead, which may not accomplish the purpose. We can "unmigrate" the dips seen in the well to see where to look on a seismic section for reflections from any particular part of the subsurface (Fig. 46). Consider the deepest dip in the well and where to look to see a reflection from the same part of the subsurface that the well saw. If the seismic line approaches the well from the up-dip directions, we will not look

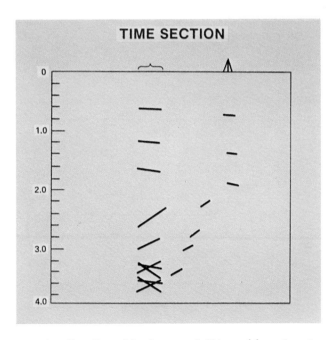

Fig. 46. "Unmigration" of well data of Fig. 44, showing where seismic data need to be recorded to map the same subsurface as sampled by the well. (From Sheriff, 1978.)

at this region if the seismic line merely tied the wellhead. If we approach
the well along the strike rather than in the dip direction, we do not want to
tie the wellhead at all but rather run our line some distance down-dip from
the well. My objective is to emphasize that you must consider where seismic
data are reflected from, when trying to relate seismic data to well data.
The exact way to program a seismic-well tie, of course, depends on the
particular local conditions, the amount of dip, what you are trying to tie it
to, and various other aspects. Basically, the problem is simply geometry.

Fig. 47 shows a model of a box sitting on a plane. The projection of
two seismic lines are also shown: one line goes across the box and the other
is to the side of the box. So far we have assumed that reflections involve
reflecting points; a more correct picture is reflecting regions. A fairly
sizable portion of a reflecting interface is involved in any observation of a
reflection. The area involved is called the "Fresnel zone" and its
dimensions are fairly large, perhaps a quarter of a mile across for shallow
reflectors and over a mile across for deep ones. The outline of the Fresnel
zone for one location is dotted in. A portion of the region laps onto the
box, and on the seismic line (lower portion of Fig. 48) we see a reflection
from the box even though no reflecting points lie on the box. The upper

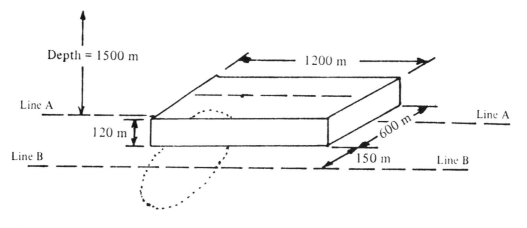

Fig. 47. Model of a box sitting on a plane. (Courtesy Geoquest.)

portion of Fig. 48 shows the line that goes across the box. The reflection from the plane approaches the box from one side, then the reflection jumps up on top of the box, and on the other side of the box the reflection drops down to the plane again. In addition we see diffractions from the discontinuities. The fact that reflections in the actual earth involve large portions of reflectors rather than simply points is an important aspect to keep in mind when interpreting seismic sections.

III. <u>Evidence of Faulting</u>

We now consider evidences of faulting of seismic lines:

(1) Abrupt termination of reflections, especially after migration.

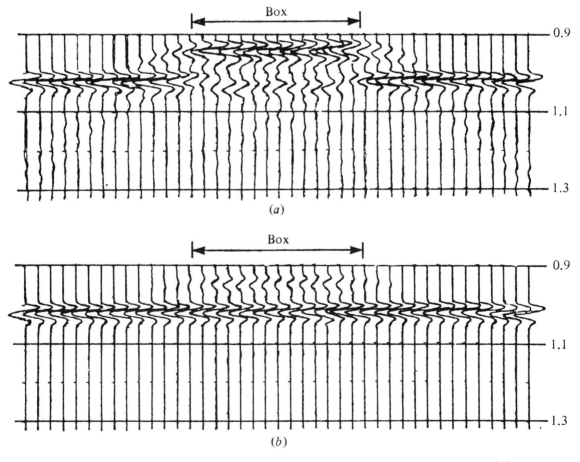

Fig. 48. Seismic lines shot over the model shown in Fig. 47. (a) Line A across the top of the box; (b) Line B on the plane to the side of the box. (Courtesy Geoquest.)

(2) Diffractions associated with fault terminations.

(3) Changes in actual dip associated with the fault; sometimes flattening, sometimes steepening. Depending on
the nature of the fault, real changes in dip rate occur
near the fault and sometimes for appreciable distances
away from the fault; such changes include drag and
rollover.

(4) Distorted dips seen through the fault. A fault juxtaposes different parts of the earth against each other
along a fault plane; that is, it juxtaposes different
velocities. Therefore, raypaths passing through the
fault plane are bent according to Snell's law by
the change in velocity at the fault plane. At different
places along a fault plane the change is
different, sometimes from lower to higher velocity and
sometimes from higher to lower. Since the contrast
changes both in magnitude and sign, raypaths are
bent in different manners as they pass through the
fault plane. This distorts the apparent dip for
events that are below the fault plane, and the distortions are
sometimes in one direction and sometimes in the other.

(5) Cutout of coherent events beneath the fault plane. We
normally recognize reflections by seeing the same phase
on adjacent seismic traces, but if adjacent raypaths
encounter different velocity contrasts at the fault and
are bent by different amounts, the distortions may be
so rapid that they destroy the sense of coherency of
reflections.

(6) Displacement of correlations across the fault. Sometimes

reflections with distinct character are offset on opposite sides of a fault and sometimes the overall reflection pattern shifts, even where distinctive reflections cannot be correlated across the fault. For example, belts of reflections or belts which are almost reflection-free may correlate even where individual reflections cannot be correlated.

(7) Fault-plane reflections. Such reflections probably occur more often than we recognize. Reflections from steeply dipping fault planes are apt to be missed because their evidences occur so far from the fault plane, their travel times are too long, and our recording-system directivity discriminates against them. Fault-plane reflections also may not have constant character.

(8) Misties. When we follow an event around a loop of a seismic grid and return to a point that is either higher or lower, we may have crossed a fault at two different locations with different amounts of throw. If faults had constant throw then misties would not result from unrecognized fault crossings, but most faults change throw laterally along the fault. Such evidences were especially important in the older days before we had the good quality record sections we have today.

A model of a simple fault is shown in Fig. 49. It is a simple vertical step. We see the reflection from the upthrown and downthrown blocks and diffractions from the upper and lower termination points. Note the continuity of amplitude between reflections and diffractions.

We cannot locate a fault by a sharp change in the amplitude nor by a sharp change in the wave shape, because the reflections are continuous with diffractions. Some interesting properties of diffractions also show, such as symmetry of the diffraction amplitude about the point on

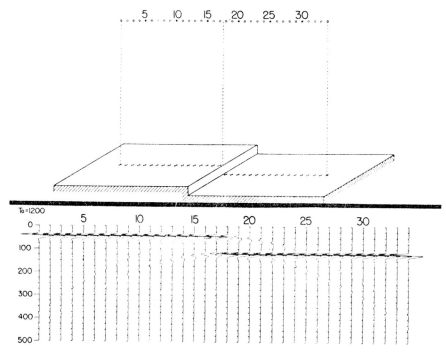

Fig. 49. Seismic model and section across it. (From Hilterman, 1970.)

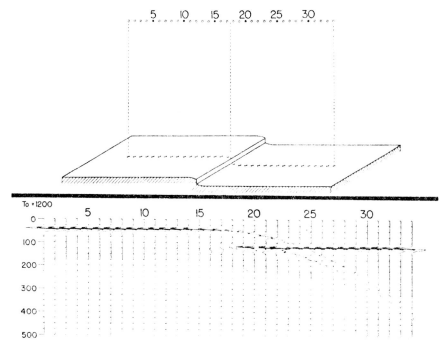

Fig. 50. Seismic model and section across it. (From Hilterman, 1970.)

the diffraction curve to which the reflection is tangent, inversion of
polarity of the diffraction at this point, etc.

The model in Fig. 49 was simple and regular so the features associated with the fault are fairly straightforward. However, this model is
varied slightly in Fig. 50 by adding drag to the fault. This
changes the picture significantly, producing slight synclinal curvature in the downthrown block and distorting the amplitude distribution.
Be cautious when developing criteria from simple models;
seemingly minor variations may significantly change criteria.

A series of faults with increasing amounts of throw produced the
section shown in Fig. 51. The amount of throw on each fault is
labeled in terms of the dominant wavelength. We earlier stated a
resolvable-limit criteria of approximately one-fourth wavelength. One
would probably pick the faults where the throw is a one-fourth wavelength
or greater, but might easily miss the faults whose throw is smaller than
one-fourth wavelength. Note that there are evidences for the smaller
faults. Even the fault with only one-sixteenth wavelength throw produces a

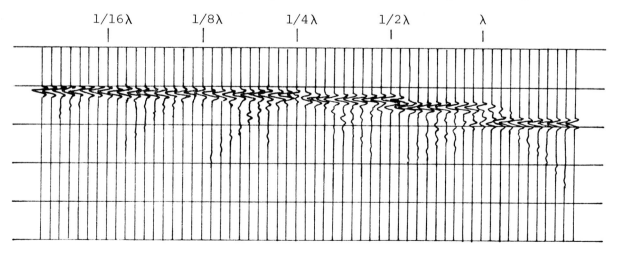

Fig. 51. Series of faults with increasing amounts of throw. The throw
on the faults is indicated in terms of the dominant wavelength. (From
Sheriff and Geldart, 1982.)

diffraction and the arrival time on the upthrown side is measurably
smaller than the arrival time on the downthrown side. However, it is
easy to miss, particularly with actual seismic data where noise and
other events and conflicts exist.

In many areas such as the Gulf Coast, compaction affects faults and
their evidences. To illustrate this (Fig. 52), assume a thickness of
about 606 m (2000 ft) of shale at the surface of the earth which is
faulted by a 50 degree fault. Then imagine the section buried to about
1818 m (6000 ft) deep with no additional fault movement involved, merely
by piling additional sediments on top. The shale had a fairly low
velocity when near the surface, possibly about 1667 m/sec (5500 ft/sec),
so the two-way travel time through the 606 m (2000 ft) of thickness was
0.727 seconds. After it is buried to a depth of 1909 m (6300 ft), its
vertical dimension is charged whereas its horizontal dimension is the
same, so the dip of the fault has actually changed and is now 40.5 de-

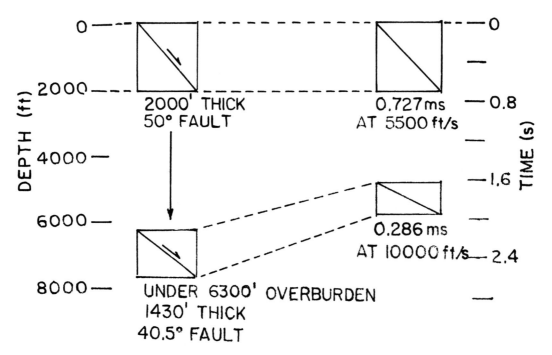

Fig. 52. Effect of compaction and seismic velocity on fault plane dip.
(After Sheriff, 1978.)

grees. Compaction thus has the effect of flattening the fault plane simply because of the vertical squeezing. The compacted section has increased velocity to perhaps 3030 m/sec (10,000 ft/sec), so that the travel time through it is smaller, probably less than 0.300 seconds. The apparent change in thickness on a seismic section is exaggerated. While the shale is actually thinner (70% of original thickness), the seismic section shows it as much thinner (40%). The normal increase of seismic velocity with depth creates apparent concave-upward fault-plane curvature. Even a planar fault appears to be curved in a concave-upward fashion and often the velocity effect merely accentuates real concave-upward curvature. Faults which grew contemporaneous with deposition and/or faults which sole-out into a bedding plane have initial concave-upward curvature. To this we must add the effects of compaction and the effects of velocity, all of which tend to make apparent curvature in a concave-upward sense.

Fig. 53 shows a fault-plane reflection from a model fault. The fault-plane reflection changes wave shape along the fault because the contrasts across the fault vary. Since in some places the higher velocity is upthrown and at other places downthrown, the reflection polarity changes. The reflection amplitude also changes because of the changing velocity contrast. Thus a fault-plane reflection is apt to be quite irregular and therefore difficult to pick. The fault is not located along the fault-plane reflection; it can probably be best located from the diffractions associated with the fault, as shown in Fig. 54, through the crests of the diffraction curves.

The seismic section in Fig. 55 is in the overthrust belt. High-velocity rocks are thrust from the left side. The situation is somewhat similar to the model shown in Fig. 2, except that the wedge of

high velocity is overthrust rather than the result of an unconformity.

A well at the left end of the section cuts the thrust plane and finds

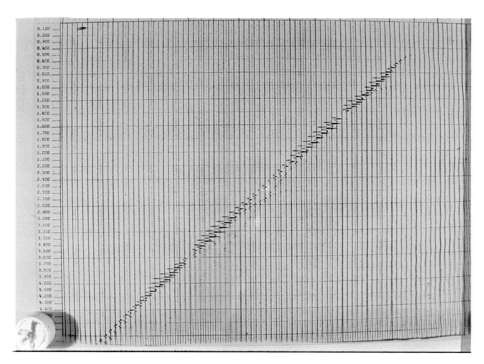

Fig. 53. Fault-plane reflection. Note changes in amplitude and polarity because of changes in the acoustic impedence contrast at the fault plane. (From Sheriff, 1978.)

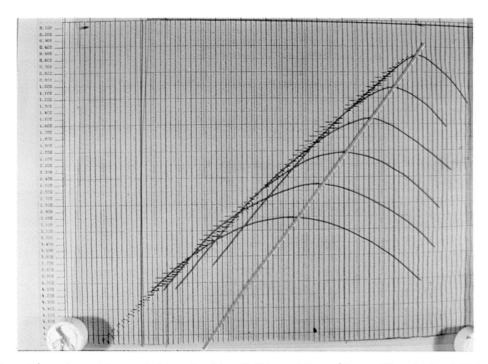

Fig. 54. Location of the fault of Fig. 53. (From Sheriff, 1978.)

repeated section. We believe the bedding below the thrust is relatively undeformed. The changes in sub-thrust reflection arrival time probably are velocity distortions, because travel time through the high-velocity thrust plate is lessened. There is probably no fault involved in the subthrust reflections, and the events which look like diffractions are probably phantom diffractions that do not represent discontinuity in the associated reflectors. They are distortion effects produced by the shallower velocity changes.

Fig. 56 is a plot of the instantaneous phase for seismic data offshore Louisiana. Phase does not contain any amplitude information but gives the sense of continuity or of discontinuity. A phase display helps isolate and locate faults.

Other measurements ("attributes") are made from seismic data and displayed to help understand faults. Figs. 57 and 58 show color-

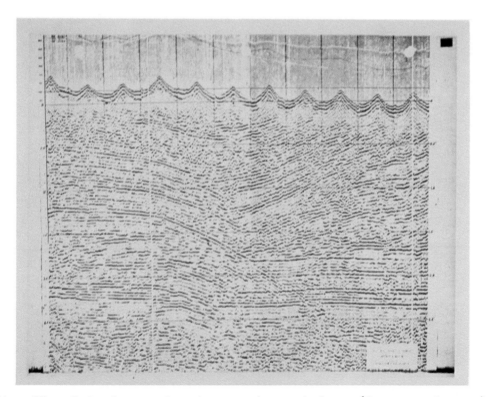

Fig. 55.   Seismic section in overthrust belt.   (Courtesy Amoco.)

coded measurements of the amplitude of the envelope and instantaneous

frequency for a seismic line offshore Alaska (instantaneous frequency

is the derivative of the instantaneous phase). Instantaneous frequency

depends on the manner in which component seismic reflections interfere;

it is nearly constant along the bedding when the reflection se-

quence is the same. It tends to characterize the sequence and thus is a

useful correlation tool, often aiding in correlation across faults. It

is also a hydrocarbon indicator, a low-frequency shadow often

found immediately under a hydrocarbon accumulation. The fault is ob-

vious. The high-amplitude event indicated by the bright red-orange

color is an unconformity, illustrating again that unconformities often

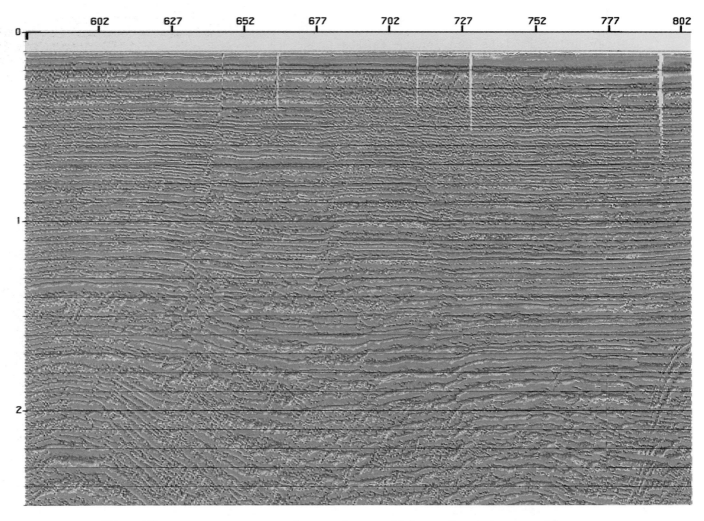

Fig. 56. Instantaneous phase plot, offshore Louisiana. (Courtesy
Seiscom-Delta.)

are among our strongest reflectors. The changes along the unconformity
tell that the contrast there differs, in this case mainly because the
section below the unconformity changes. The instantaneous frequency
display shown in Fig. 58 shows features that appear different from what is
most evident on the amplitude display. In the upper part (A), the
overall instantaneous frequency character is nearly the same on
both sides of the fault, telling us that the sequence of reflection
contrasts is the same. The fault was post depositional in this region,
so that both sides involve the same reflectors with the same thickness-
es. However, immediately above the unconformity (section B) this is not
true; here the pattern on the upthrown side differs from that on the
downthrown side. The fault grew during the deposition of those
sediments and they are thicker downthrown, so their component reflec-

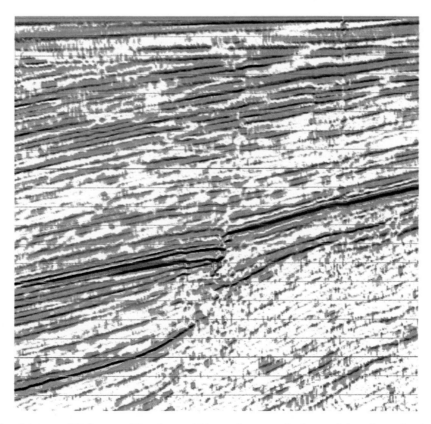

Fig. 57. Section offshore Alaska with color-coded amplitude of the
envelope overprinted on seismic section. The bright colors (red, orange,
yellow) indicate strong reflections; the weak colors (blue, green)
indicate weaker reflections. (Courtesy Seiscom-Delta.)

tions interfere differently and produce a different frequency pattern.

A seismic line in south Texas is shown in Fig. 59. Faulting is critical to accumulation in this area. This section was processed with a coherency filter, which improved the sense of continuity of reflections but degraded the faulting evidences. Amplitude (Fig. 60) and instantaneous frequency displays (Fig. 61) clarify the faulting picture. The throw on the faults is seen by offsets of patterns, which are sometimes clearest on the amplitudes display and sometimes clearest on the frequency display.

A growth fault model was used to generate Fig. 62. The bedding attitudes differ in the different fault blocks, because of growth on different faults at different times and because of the rotation assoc-

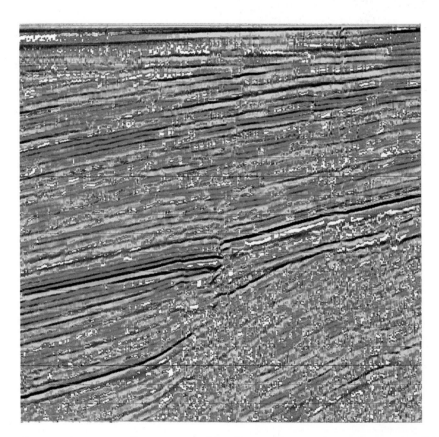

Fig. 58. Instantaneous frequency display of section shown in Fig. 57. Bright colors (orange, yellow) indicate low frequencies; greens and blues indicate higher frequencies. (Courtesy Seiscom-Delta.)

iated with curved (listric) fault planes. Reverse faults could be drawn
(incorrectly) through the reflection terminations. The differences in
the dip of different reflector segments caused their reflections to
be seen at different distances from their actual locations and sometimes
makes them seem associated with the wrong fault blocks. The correct
interpretation locates normal faults through the diffraction crests.

A prograding section builds out over an underlying shelf with
little faulting in Fig. 63, but a system of growth faults develops
beyond the shelf edge where the underlying "foundation" disappeared.
Fault interpretation requires a sense of structural style. Structural

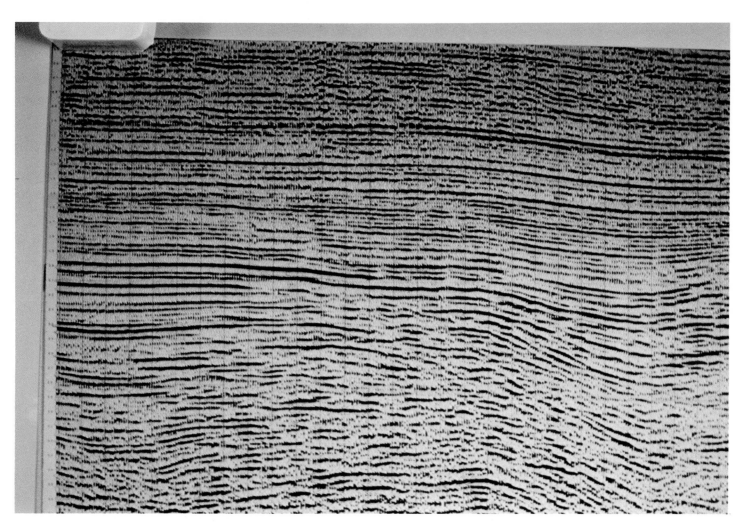

Fig. 59. Seismic line in south Texas. (Courtesy Seiscom-Delta.)

style involves understanding the system of forces that affected the
rocks we are dealing with. The form and manner of deformation differs
as the stress systems differ and as the nature of the rocks differ.

Fig. 60. Line shown in Fig. 59 color-coded for amplitude of the envelope, with faults interpreted. (Courtesy Seiscom-Delta.)

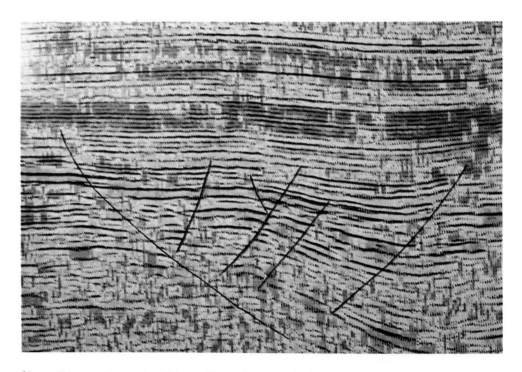

Fig. 61. Line shown in Fig. 59 color-coded for instantaneous frequency.
(Courtesy Seiscom-Delta.)

Interpretations which imply inconsistency of stresses are not right. Structural-style concepts tell the types of features to look for and what the faults probably do. You often must decide between continuing a fault down through basement, soleing it out as bedding-plane slip, or having it die in a flow feature.

Fig. 64 shows a shelf edge beyond which the section drops down along a listric fault. The rotation on the fault plane stretched the upper portion and produced secondary antithetic faulting.

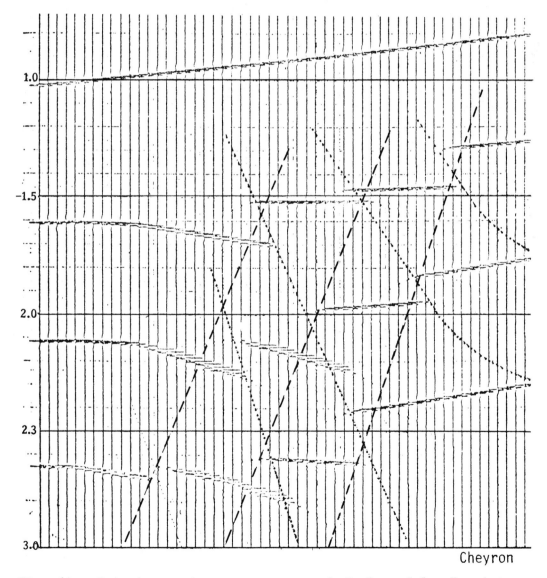

Cheyron

Fig. 62. Seismic section across a growth-fault model. Two interpretations are shown: (a) as reverse faults (dotted lines), and (b) as normal faults (dashed lines). (From Sheriff, 1978.)

The high-resolution section of Fig. 65 has appreciable high-frequency content, up to about 200 Hz. As a result we can see very small faulting. The fault marked has a throw of only a few feet, and yet it shows clearly. Much effort is devoted to increasing the high frequency content of seismic data. Increasing the frequency shortens the wavelength and allows us to resolve smaller features.

A number of faults show on Fig. 66. Some of these are marked (along with several vertical disruptions of alignments indicated by arrows at the bottom of the section). The vertical alignments do not indicate faults, but result from distortions associated with the bending

Fig. 63. Portion of seismic section built out over a shelf edge. (Courtesy Exxon.)

of raypaths in crossing the fault planes. These near-vertical alignments are often associated with fault cuts of prominent reflections. We
are generally suspicious of vertical patterns on seismic sections. Most
geologic features do not occur in a vertical pattern, whereas near-
surface effects and many defects in seismic recording or processing do
produce vertical patterns.

Only one fault is required in the center of Fig. 67, because only
one set of diffractions is seen (except for those associated with
the fault scarp which has eroded back). One might be tempted to interpret two faults here.

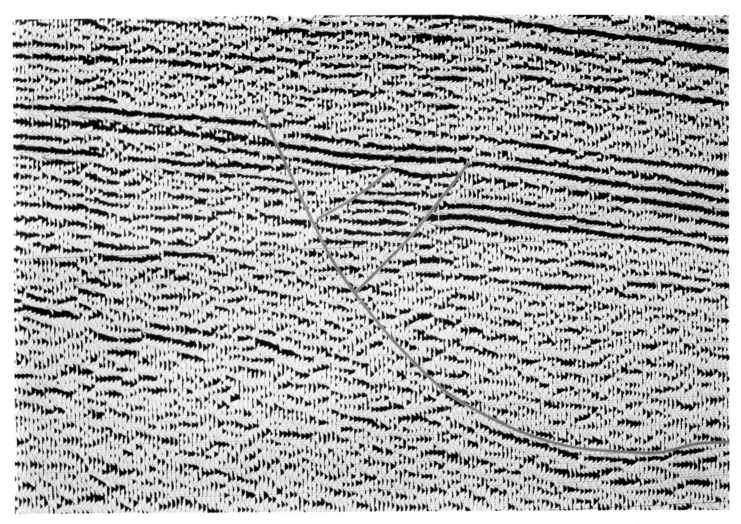

Fig. 64. Listric Faulting at a shelf edge. (Courtesy Seiscom-Delta.)

Another section in the overthrust belt is seen in Fig. 68. It shows many of the same features seen in Fig. 55. High-velocity rocks are thrust in from the left of the section and the lateral velocity variation produces distortions in the deeper data. As in Fig. 55, there seems to be another thrust in front of the main high-velocity thrust, and this forward thrust apparently involves lower-than-normal velocities and a slight velocity sag in the underlying, continuous reflectors.

The top of a triangle laid on the section in Fig. 69 approximately

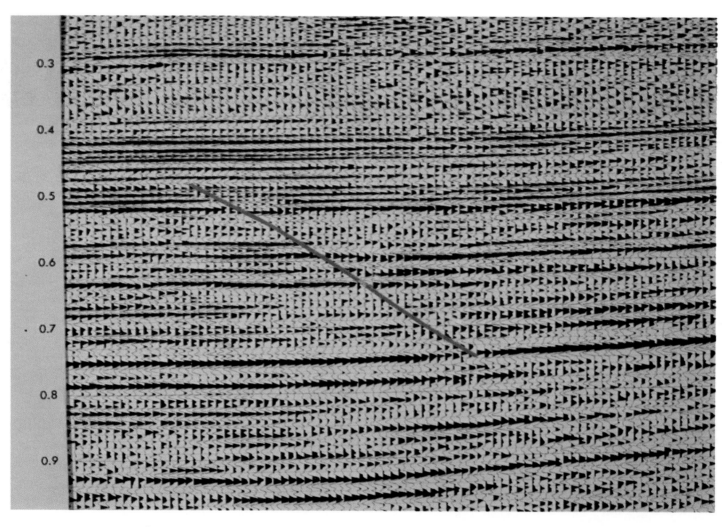

Fig. 65. High-resolution section allowing a very small fault to be seen. (Courtesy Seiscom-Delta.)

marks a fault. A variety of types of evidence lie along it: termin-

ation of reflections, offset of reflections, changes in amplitude,

changes in frequency, phasing of various types, anomalous dips, etc.

Fig. 70 shows folding and faulting, results of high-angle reverse

faulting of the basement. The sediments are mainly young, relatively

unconsolidated, and sufficiently plastic to have yielded by folding in

some places, by minor flowing in some, and by faulting in some. The

high-angle reverse faulting produces a secondary antithetic normal

fault.

Faulting does not cause all strange features on seismic sections.

Fig. 71 shows predominately gentle dips, cut by a family of

steeper dips, that seem to roll over (the data in the crestal area

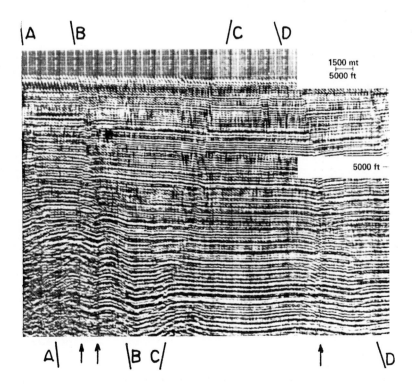

Fig. 66. Section showing several normal faults (A,B,C,D) and also several vertical alignments which do not indicate faults. (From Tucker and
Yorsten, 1973.)

deteriorate in quality). The family of steep dips comes from
the side and is an example of side swipe. This section is in
Mississippi and a salt dome lies to one side of the line.

There is a temptation to interpret Fig. 72 as a small grabin, but
the bounding faults are too nearly vertical and you must be suspicious
of vertical alignments. A change in the sea-floor reflection is associated with velocity distortion. Another viewpoint is that the
data are improperly time-shifted and we might call this a statics error,
having not removed the distorting effects of the near-surface velocity
variations.

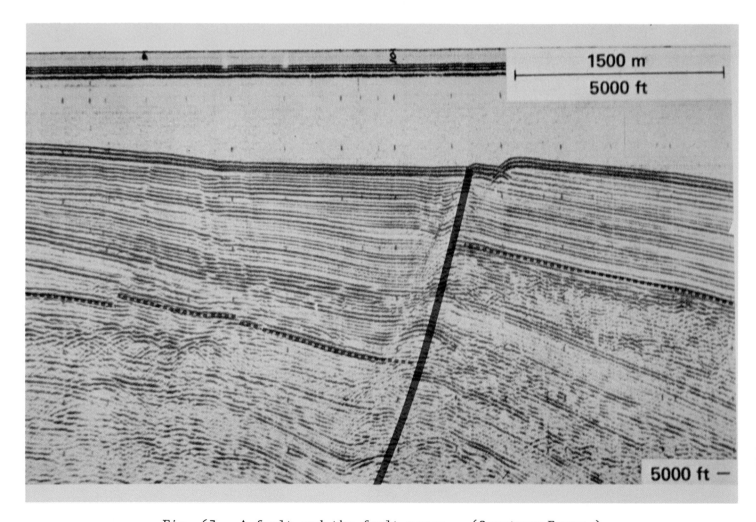

Fig. 67. A fault and the fault scarp. (Courtesy Exxon.)

Fig. 73 is difficult to interpret sensibly because the line changes direction by a small amount. As a result, you see different components of the dip. The degradation of quality in the middle involves incorrect normal-moveout removal because source-hydrophone distances were affected by the line bending but allowance was not made in the processing. Consequently, data in this region were not stacked optimally.

Acknowledgements

I wish to thank the Dallas Geological Society for allowing the American Association of Petroleum Geologists (AAPG) to tape my presentation, Terry Hillman of Science-Thru-Media for her strenuous efforts to make a good tape-slide presentation and for considering (though not always accommodating) my desires to make changes, and Ron Hart and the AAPG for their patience while I prepared the written manuscript.

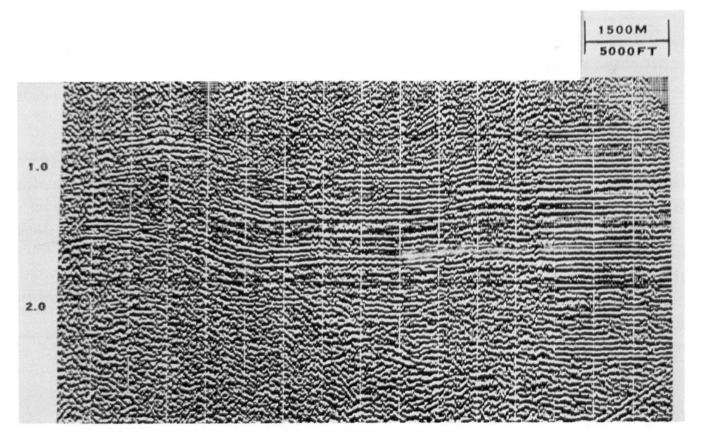

Fig. 68.   Section in overthrust belt. (From Tucker and Yorsten, 1973.)

I also wish to thank the organizations who permitted me to show their sections and work: Society of Exploration Geophysicists, Seiscom Delta, Amoco, Chevron, Conoco, and Exxon.

Thanks also goes to colleagues who developed or helped develop the ideas discussed here: M.T. Taner and Fred Hilterman in particular, and to my wife, Margaret, for her help, patience, encouragement, understanding, and heckling.

Fig. 69. Section across a normal fault. (Courtesy Seiscom-Delta.)

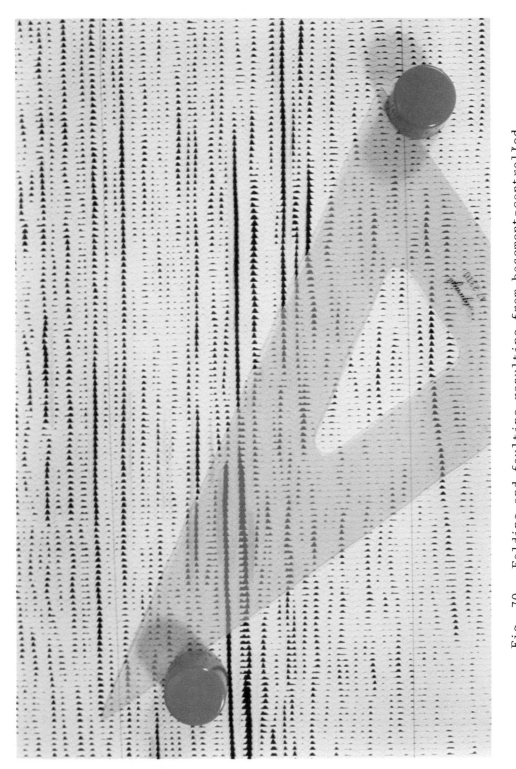

Fig. 70. Folding and faulting resulting from basement-controlled reverse faulting. (Courtesy Seiscom-Delta.)

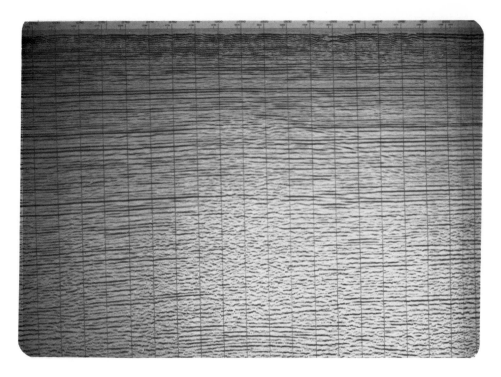

Fig. 71. Section showing side swipe from a salt dome to the side of the line. (Courtesy Seiscom-Delta.)

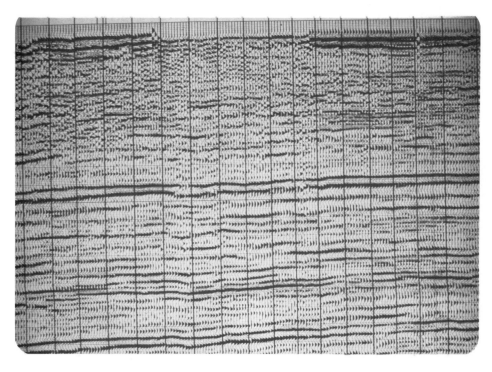

Fig. 72. Section showing effects of changes in the near-surface. (Courtesy Seiscom-Delta.)

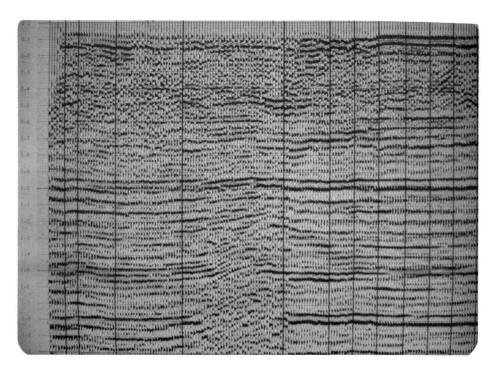

Fig. 73. Section involving a change in direction. (Courtesy Seiscom-Delta.)